Jim Flynn (signature)

Stranger to the System

Life Portraits of a New York City Homeless Community

Collected by Jim Flynn
Illustrated by Nelson Hall

CURBSIDE PRESS
NEW YORK
2002

Poetry and portraits by Nelson Hall reprinted
with permission

Photos by Clayton Patterson, Bob Arahood, Jeff Owen, Skunk,
and Monte reprinted with permission

Personal testimonies printed with permission of the speakers.
Some names and identifying details have been changed
at the subjects' request.

Published by Curbside Press, New York, NY
www.curbsidepress.com

Book composition and production by Palabris, et al., New York
www.palabris.com

Distributed by the people of the streets of New York

Printed in the United States of America

ISBN 0-9741559-0-X
2 4 6 8 10 9 7 5 3 1

Book design by Liz Polizzi and Jim Flynn
Cover design by Nick Polizzi and the Great Spirit

Official theme song "Goya 101" by Ish Marquez
listen at
www.artists.mp3s.com/artists/171/lonesome_crew.html

for Walt and Eleanor
and all the teachers who inspired me to
learn outside the classroom

After reading most of Matthew
I smiled and then I laughed.
I held my glance a second longer
when I held a blade of grass
And since words were only breaths
All I could do was nod.
We were standing on one corner
both looking at and praying to one God.

Turner Cody

Contents

In Search of a Real New York   1

History of Tompkins Square Park   3

The Living Room   4

     Phillip 6
     Sweet Leif 22
     The Chess Master 34
     Jerome 39
     Vinny 48
     Nancy Lane Smith 55
     RinoThunder 64
     Gray Wolf 74
     John Connors 83
     Nelson Hall 88
     The Ligher Side 116
     Snapshots 120

Crusty Punk Lane   127

     Anna 130
     Gypsy 143
     Stephanie 150
     Bolt 165
     Bolt and Stephanie 184
     James Carter 199
     Skunk 210
     George 218
     The Lighter Side 230
     Snapshots 232

The Outskirts   244

Lawrence LaDouceur...................................244
Cheneke...256
Snapshots 260

A Helping Hand   269

Street Life Ministries
Reverend David Van Fleet 269
Lower East Side Harm Reduction Center /
Needle Exchange
Raquel Algarin.......................................270
Picture the Homeless
Anthony Williams.................................... 271
Gene Rice and Warren Prince..................... 272
Grand Central Neighborhood Coalition / BIGnews
Ron Grunberg...273

Epilogues   275

The Antiriot of August 2002...................... . 283
Life Portraits...288

Resurrection   299

—Nelson Hall

About Curbside Press................................302
About the Author.....................................304
Aknowledgements....................................306

Listen to audio excerpts from these stories at

curbsidepress.com

In Search of a Real New York

Fed up with the transparent hipsters on the downtown bar scene, in spring of 2001 I set out to collect the life stories of the people sleeping on the streets around Tompkins Square. I passed by the park a few times a week, mostly in the evening, and chatted with the diverse tribe of people who frequented the benches. If the conversation proved interesting, I'd ask for permission to tape record. There were a few who rejected my offer, but most were eager to proclaim their story to the world.

These volunteers represent only a microscopic sliver of the homeless people living in New York City. Many of these untold thousands* successfully hide the outward signs of their dilemma while struggling to remedy their situation from inside the system. I did not find many of these people in Tompkins Square Park.

This anthology focuses mainly (but not exclusively) on people who are "visually homeless"—those who can be seen sleeping on public benches, sorting through dumpsters, or begging for money. Most have been living on the street for an extended period of time, and even if willing, few possess the identification required to receive services from programs. Some have completely given up hope of ever conforming to an acceptable role

*In winter of 2003 city homeless shelters served up to 38,000 people per night, a 24% increase over the previous year. It is impossible to accurately determine the number of people on the streets who do not seek services.

in our money driven culture. Environmental factors and internal struggles have forced these fellow citizens to pursue their lives on a separate playing field. Although both worlds intertwine at the edges, they remain Strangers to the System.

While editing these interviews into narrative form, I found it necessary to alter much of the syntax and chronological sequence of the original recordings. Some names have been changed to protect personal privacy, but none of the content that I have rendered is fictitious. All but two of the subjects had the opportunity to listen to the first draft of their story and help me alter it according to their wishes.

"We are all individuals. The only one you can correct is yourself." —Rino Thunder

This book is not a statistical compendium, nor is it a soapbox for ideological propaganda. These are merely some words that were exchanged between friends on park benches. Rather than dwell on the details of my own experiences, I leave you to reap the insights and emotions of your own harvest.

"Cause we love it—when there's plenty of it."
—The Reverend Doctor Daddy Max

History of Tompkins Square Park

"If all the ghosts came back to Tompkins, the place would be so packed you couldn't even walk."

— James Carter

Tompkins Square is a ten-and-a-half-acre public park squeezed between Manhattan's Lower East Side and East Village. Its bench-lined pathways and grassy fields have served as a refreshing refuge for generations of immigrants seeking a foothold on the American Dream. Many of the events that would define their struggle took place inside these fences, and the park's history is a rich chronicle of class tensions in New York City. In it's 166 years the park has seen six full-scale riots, with the last two occurring in 1988 and 1991. Between these two uprisings the park was covered with the makeshift shelters of hundreds of homeless people.

Although recent years have witnessed tremendous economic growth in the area, the community of homeless people who continue to spend their days in the park serve as a lingering reminder of the neighborhood's turbulent past and a visible testament to the dilemmas that continue to plague our city.

To read Jim Flynn's full length History of Tompkins Square Park please visit www.curbsidepress.com.

The Living Room

If Tompkins Square is the living room of the Lower East Side, then the bench-lined path across from Avenue A is the Living Room of Tompkins Square. This heavily trafficked stretch is a center of interaction for a variety of neighborhood dwellers. Stiffly garbed briefcase wielders tap at two-thousand-dollar laptop computers, while the next bench over a grizzled senior citizen diligently attempts to dislodge a copy of yesterday's *Post* from a gizmo-laden baby stroller. Babushka-clad Polish women knit with steady hand against the echo of congas, and gray-haired strategists stare at the chessboard with fierce contemplation. The Living Room is the crossroads of urban America, and an eager soul seeking conversation is not to be denied.

At the height of the summer, I would say that there are probably a total of fifty "regulars" at the Living Room who do not return home to an apartment once the park closes. Although there is a diverse spectrum within this population, it is not unreasonable to say that most of them are alcoholics. Many of my interviews are conducted while the subject slowly numbs the senses.

The issue of open container creates a constant cat-and-mouse game with patrolling squad cars from the 9th Precinct. Although tempers occasionally flare during these encounters, most of the regulars accept them with grumbling resignation. My own interactions with the police are also strained. Officers often ask me to open the lid on my coffee cup only to find coffee. One night three officers surround me and search my pockets for drugs. Despite my anger at these events, I must also commend the 9th Precinct for it's alert response to medical emergencies. Whenever I call 911 for people who are having seizures, the officers arrive within a few minutes.

The most fascinating aspect of the Living Room is watching the interactions between people sleeping on the streets and those with an apartment in the area. Not all of the regulars are homeless. A man named Joe often invites people to sleep on his roof on Avenue A. There is also a Jewish lady named Carla who chats vigorously as weathered hands caress her poodle. Another neighbor, Diane, brings bags of food. From time to time former homeless people return to the park and offer encouragement to their friends on the street.

As autumn fades into winter, the regulars at the Living Room gradually begin to disperse. Some disappear, while others take up residence in the Second Avenue subway station. When springtime arrives, old and new faces return to these benches to lay the foundation for a new community.

Phillip

Queens, New York 1950

Phillip's soft smiling face is a constant presence in the Living Room. The only time he leaves the park is when it closes, and even then he rarely ventures more than a few blocks away. Immersed in a torrential thunder of non-stop talkers, Phillip is content to sit back with a beer and let the world roll by. His mellow nature is respected by all, and his easy laughter has gained him many friends. Although I've heard people jokingly refer to Phillip as "Uncle Remus," they mostly just call him Pops.

Phillip sleeps on the sidewalk in front of the 7A Restaurant with a fairly consistent group of old-timers. His stationary nature makes him a favorite when people need someone to watch their bags. Phillip takes pride in this role, and whenever I run across the street to the bodega, he insists that I leave my briefcase with him for safekeeping.

I grew up in an apartment on 75th Street in Far Rockaway. It was a small family—just my mother and father, my four brothers, and my sister. I guess my childhood was pretty regular. Me and my brothers was always running around playing cowboys and Indians with the other kids in the neighborhood. I had a cowboy hat and a Fanning six-shooter cap gun. Bap. Bap. Bap. We played crack top, scully and some other games. You don't know scully? It's like lowlies, where you get down and try to spin the top into different boxes. Kids don't do that today. Now the kids be sitting inside with the video games. It was different then. People were very close back in the day. Everybody on the block knew everybody's child. You disrespect Miss So and So, you come home and the message is already there. "Take your pants off son."

My father hustled different jobs doing construction and cleaning. He didn't have much formal education, but he was sharp about business. The good thing was that he always paid the rent. The bad thing was that he was more or less an alcoholic. Things got ugly whenever he drank. If he had a hard day at work, he'd contain it all day, but then he'd just come home and get messed up on Benzedrine and alcohol. Sometimes he'd hit my mother. When I first started realizing what was going on, I was just a six-year-old kid, and there was nothing I could do but sit there and cry for my mother. That's why I never did that with my own families. I never beat a woman in my life.

There was two parts of the Rockaways, the all-black part and the mixed part. I actually lived just inside the mixed part. It was a nice neighborhood, and I got along with the white kids. They liked having me around. First time I ever got drunk was with white boys. We were sitting down in the park, and this white boy said it was time I started drinking Schlitz. At first I couldn't get the taste down, but after a few I started liking it. I ended up getting pretty ripped, and they had to carry me home. You should have seen my father's face when he opened the door and saw two white boys holding me up. I was so drunk he had to wait for the next day to blast me out.

I wasn't a troubled kid. It was just that I had a lot of friends who were troubled kids. First time I stole something was in 1962. Me and my friend Eddie was needing to be getting wood to make a scooter, so we jumped over a fence into the neighbor's yard. I was getting up the wood, but all the sudden Eddie started killing the chickens in the pen. I don't know what this boy was thinking. He was making so much noise that the police showed up. The only thing I got was a JD (*juvenile delinquent*) card, but when my mother and father was through with me, my behind was so sore that I couldn't come out for three days. THREE DAYS.

Getting my ass whipped didn't really make me wanna stop stealing, it just made me wanna make sure I didn't get caught. When I was fourteen I started hanging out with a bunch of cats called the Robin Hood Gang, because we was always robbin the hood. There was about fifteen of us, and we'd just go out stealing at night. One weekend one of my friends decided to try and snatch a pocketbook. He got caught, but I got taken in too. When they took me to the station, I wouldn't tell the police who really snatched the pocketbook. They had a lawyer talk to me and everything, but I still wouldn't tell. That was against the code.

The judge ended up sending me to Warwick State Training Facility. My father really tore me up before I left. I thought it was gonna be like jail, but it really wasn't that bad. You weren't behind bars. It was actually a lot of open fields. You'd spend three months in the dorm, and then if you got gold stars, they'd give you passes to go home for the weekend. I liked it so much more back in Queens. Back there I had an exciting life with partying. There wasn't that much excitement in the boys' home, because you couldn't drink there, and remember, it was all boys. (*laughs*) After nine months I went back home for good.

That summer was when I really started to become a young man. I started dressing more slick—Kangos, bellbottoms, leather shoes. Instead of hanging out in my own part of town, I started going over to the other side. That's where the girls was at. We used to have big parties when somebody's parents would go away for the weekend. We had blue-light parties, red-light parties, and green-light parties. Blue-light is like when you dance real slow with the girl and hold her. Green-light is like when you have fast action on the dance floor and a lot of conversation. A red-light party was basically anything goes—raid the building, run through the house.

When I went back to regular school that September, they put me in the slow class. I didn't like that. It was like kindergarten. I told my mother about it, and she went into the school and said that she wanted me in a regular class. They wouldn't do that. I knew I didn't have no place being in the CR and D class, so I went to the office and asked for my working papers and inoculations. The principal asked me if I was sure I wanted to do it, and I said yes. I didn't see why they had to put me in that class.

I found a job in the Neighborhood Youth Core cleaning up the parks after the dances. I made $32.92 a week, but I had to give my mother five bucks a week to help out with the rent. I also had to save money so that when I went to a party, I'd have a few dollars in my pocket. That was a good time for me. I was a single young man, and I could enjoy myself. That's the year that I met Jessica.

It started when I was hanging around outside of the liquor store, talking to this older guy in a wheelchair. He kind of took a liking to me and told me that he wanted me to meet his daughter. I wasn't doing nothing, so I said OK. We went back to his place, and there she was, Jessica. She was big boned, but she had a baby face. Right away I liked her a lot. She didn't like to be hit on, so it took me a while to get to her. I used to stop by once in a while, and then I asked her to be my girlfriend. We'd go to Coney Island and I'd buy her little trinkets, watches and rings. My favorite was when we used to go pick up some wood and relax in front of the wood stove. We were close.

Everything was going pretty good in my life. Then, one day in July, Jessica comes to me and says she gotta tell me something. From the look in her eye I knew it wasn't good. She was pregnant. Oh Lord! I didn't know what to do. I took Jessica and her father home to meet my family. Her father and my father talked. Then my father called me into the room. He looked at me and asked if I had twenty-five dollars. I said yeah. Then he told me to give it to Jessica. He said that I had to give her twenty-five dollars each week. I had to get a night job in a paper factory from five till twelve every weekday. That was the end of me just being a kid out to enjoy myself.

I kept visiting Jessica at her parents' house when I could. See, back in those days you couldn't live together. At 8 o'clock in the evening, her parents would tell her that it was time for her company to leave. One night, just before I had to leave, I asked her if she wanted to marry me. She said, "You don't love me, Phillip. You only asking because we have a baby." I kept trying to tell her that I loved her, but Jessica wouldn't pay it no mind. After that we broke up—but my father said I still had to pay her that twenty-five dollars a week.

After Jessica left me, I started talking to this other young lady named Janet. She had a big house, and I used to go visit her on the porch. She was tall, a little

bit on the skinny side, but she had a mind like a computer. She could talk to me about anything. We went
for walks, and I used to spend time helping her
around the house. After a few weeks, we became close.
Now, you think I woulda learnt my lesson the first
time, but I guess you could say I was a young man,
and I liked pushing the old rod. *(laughs)* You know
what I'm saying? Guess what? I found out that August
that Janet was pregnant too. When I took her to meet
my dad, he said, "I don't know what you're doing son,
but you're wearing yourself thin." He made me take
another twenty-five dollars out of my paycheck each
week and give it to Janet.

It was kind of rough when the two girls found out
about each other, because they lived right across the
street. I was worried that they was gonna fight, but all
they did was come together and hug. You know why?
Because I was taking care of both of 'em. I wasn't leaving neither one of them stressed out. At the time the
hospital charged a little under a thousand dollars for
babies. Neither one of these women would take any
welfare money, so I paid the whole thing. They were
both in the same hospital, one on the fifth floor and the
other was on the third floor. Jessica gave me a daughter, Roxanne, and Janet gave me a son, Howard.

Right after that, I asked Janet to marry me, but
she said no. She was a free spirit and didn't want
nobody to own her. What I liked about my women
was their inner strength. I saw that. They didn't
wanna get married just because of the fact that we had
children. That would have made a bad marriage.

I kept working at the factory at night and for the
park service in the day. I had to pay for the fact that
these are my kids. After I bought food, diapers, and

formula, it only left me with about twenty dollars a week for myself. It was a rough time, but all and all I enjoyed it. I had goals to work for, and it kept me pretty busy. I stayed in both Janet and Jessica's lives. Sometimes we'd all get together, and Howard and Roxanne would play. We had birthday parties with all the families. I enjoyed it even though I didn't have a lot of time for myself. I didn't hardly drink at all back then.

In 1973 my grandfather in South Carolina died. My father wanted to keep the house in the family, so I signed it over to Jessica. It was a nice two-family house with a yard. She moved down there and started working as a nurse. We stayed in touch for a while, and I sent her some money to help her pay the mortgage.

That same year, Janet and I got some money together and applied for public housing. Then me, her, and Howard moved into the Edgemere project in the Rockaways. Janet and me lived together like husband and wife. I loved her. I never hit her. I never beat her. I got frustrated at times, but my kid never went to school with black eyes or saw their mother with a busted lip.

We used to have to pay one hundred and forty dollars a month for rent. Then, the more money you made, the more money it would cost for rent. When I first went in there, it was mostly working people, as the years went on, you had more welfare recipients. At the time, welfare was only giving sixty-eight fifty a month, so you had people who made up the rent with selling food stamps. Janet never believed in public assistance, so we had to work. If we was gonna buy a TV or something, we'd never pay credit.

Coming into the seventies, I had another son with Janet named Steven. We also had another boy named

Randolph. He really wasn't my son. This lady who was a cocaine addict left him with Janet. He always used to wake us up in his sleep, because cocaine babies have a lung condition. When he got to be five or six, he started calling me Dad.

It wasn't always easy, but looking back I see that it felt good to have people need me. I did whatever I could. When my kids were young, I put money into bank accounts for each of them, so when they got of age, they had money of their own. An old Jewish woman told me to do that. My kids' lives were pretty stable. They never got into fights or drugs. They had smart mothers.

In 1979 a friend hooked me up with a custodial job at Nassau Coliseum. The money was pretty good, and I liked working just one job, but that only lasted until I got laid off in '82. After that I had to get some odds-and-ends jobs to maintain the household. I didn't want to accept welfare, so I did a lot of painting and cleaning. The money wasn't anywhere near as good, and that kind of stressed me out.

In 1983 Howard comes to me and says, Dad I got a girl pregnant. I was like oh, not again. I'm tired of that. I told him that he was gonna have to start working, so he dropped out of school completely and started driving an ambulette. He married the mother of his kids later on and went on to pass the GED. He owns his own landscaping company now, and he's doing all right. A couple years after that, Steven comes to me and says the same thing. Then he had to move out and get a job. Howard and Steven always wondered why they never had enough money to buy things for themselves, but when you have a woman and a child you have to be more giving.

I was glad to see that my kids were starting to grow up and take care of themselves. I had spent the last twenty years of my life working everyday just to put food on the table, and that was a long time for a man to give up his life. I wanted to take some time for myself, but then in 1988, Janet had a daughter named Nadine.

I stayed with Janet for another year to help her out, but she knew that I wasn't going to stick around. It was nothing that Janet did, and it was nothing that I did. I just knew that I needed to get out of New York and start seeing things for myself. We didn't have no argument. We just agreed that it would be better. Doesn't mean I didn't love her. I told her she could keep the apartment and all my stuff, and when I got myself straight, I'd come back.

Leaving that apartment was like a release, like Ahhh. I went down to the bank and took out all the money I'd been saving. I had eight thousand dollars in my pocket, and I went and bought myself a train ticket to Las Vegas. I had nothing, just the clothes on my back. If I wanted a clean shirt, I'd just buy one. I was partying and just living it up. That was like the first time in twenty years that I got to do my own thing. It felt good to have nothing to worry about.

From Las Vegas I went to South Dakota. I wanted to see the Badlands, like in all the cowboy movies. I stayed there a few months in a hotel room. There weren't too many people for me to talk to, so I started drinking. I was upset, because for all these years I had been imagining what I could do on my own, and it wasn't working out the way I planned it. After a few months I took a train to Louisiana, where I stayed with some of my cousins in the swamps.

From there I called up my mother, and she said

that Roxanne had called me from South Carolina, and she wanted to see her daddy. I hadn't seen Roxanne in years, so I got on the train and went down there. I was amazed. Roxanne was all grown up and going to school to be a nurse like her mom. The house looked brand new. They fixed it up outside and inside. They had things of their own, their own cars and whatnot. I stayed there for two weeks, but I really didn't fit in. Jessica never got remarried, but there was nothing left in our relationship. She wished me well, and I headed back to New York.

My trip lasted for seven months. I spent all my money on drinking and hotel rooms. When I got back to New York, I still wasn't ready to go back to Janet. Instead I stayed at my sister's house for about a year. She's an Evangelical Minister, and my brother-in-law is a deacon. They was always talking to me about God and life. I used to come home drunk, and they had issues with that. I couldn't have her being my mother, so I walked out of there. They got their lives. I got mine.

When I left there, I moved in with a friend in Far Rockaway for a while, then I stayed with my cousin in Brooklyn. I stayed with a couple different friends, but I got tired of being up in everybody's business. In 1990 I rented a room in a flophouse and started working odds-and-ends. That same year some guy tried to rob me, and I cut him with my knife.

They took me to trial and found me guilty. I got two years of parole. I walked away from that because my PO (parole officer) was an A hole. He said you gotta do this, do that. Now, me being a man, I don't appreciate that. My father'd died ten years before that, and I don't need no other man to tell me what I gotta do. When I skipped out on parole, I didn't have nowhere to go, so I just walked the streets in Brooklyn and Queens. I stayed out on the street for five years eating at shelters and panhandling—drinking liquor all the time. In '95 the police picked me up for open container, and they sentenced me to five years upstate for parole violation. I don't like to talk about that so much.

I ended up doing two and a half years upstairs, and then they released me to a halfway house called McCauley Mission. They were really big on religion. I stayed there for about three months. For the first month, you couldn't leave the building. It was pretty rough. Eventually, I became a security guard there. If I stayed for a few more months, they were going to put me in a program where I would have my own apartment, but I got fed up with that, and I went back out on the street.

That was when I first started living around Tompkins Square Park. Being on the streets over here is much better than being out in Brooklyn. I love the people here. You meet all types of people in this park and learn what they're about. I talk to doctors and lawyers. You meet people who have insight. I just soak it all up. It's like an education.

Phillip is the first subject that I speak with after 9/11. He greets me with a hug and tells me that during the emergency the park had turned into a free for all. People were smoking pot and shooting up right out in the open, just like the old days. Tears were shed and several of the more unstable regulars had nervous breakdowns.

As I sit down on the bench, Phillip spies a police cruiser slowly edging toward the Living Room. He quickly swallows the rest of his beer and pushes the can behind the bench. A short stocky Hispanic officer steps out of the car and scans over the people passed out on the benches. He clicks on a flashlight and calls out in a shrill voice, "All right, first we gotta get Sleeping Beauty up. Sleeping Beauty, get up!" The officer pulls the blankets off the man's head. Startled, he jerks himself upright. The officer then turns and faces Phillip. "Now I divert my attention to the very slick one. What you got under that jacket. A bomb? A bomb of alcohol? We're looking for bombs. Come on, let me see. Tick tick tick tick tick. Hurry. Hurry. What do you think I'm stupid?" Phillip lifts up his jacket. There's nothing underneath. "You're good. What about that bag? What you got in there?"

I'm just watching it for a friend, but I think it's mostly clothes.

The officer sorts through the contents of the bag. "Just want to make sure that there's nothing in here that could harm a passing child should he happen to find it." After emptying half of the contents, he finds a full a can of Budweiser, which he opens and pours on the ground. "I'll leave the can in case he wants the nickel." The officer proceeds to check the next bench where a man named Stack is passed out in the upright position. The officer routinely opens up the inside of his jacket and pats down his chest. As he leaves, "Sleeping Beauty" shouts, "Why don't you go down to the World Trade Center, bother somebody down there! Harassing me. I ain't doing shit! Yeah, the name on your badge is [Hispanic name]. But you ain't no Puerto Rican. You're white! That's what you are, a white Puerto Rican!"

That makes me angry. Much more going on in the world today than me drinking a beer in the park. He's always trying to catch me with a beer. But to hell with you, you not gonna catch me with no beer! *Phillip pulls another beer out of his jacket with a coy smile.*

I don't worry about too much. Whenever I get sick, I get an antihistamine and a cup of tea. If that doesn't work, I go to the hospital. They're my friends. They know me. I go to Bellevue, because they're the best in the world. I don't even have to show ID, because my name is registered there. But even if I didn't have that, they would still take me. Doctors, real doctors, are lifesavers. Remember they took a Hippocratic oath. They stand by that.

I try to take it slow. When I wake up, I get me a cup of coffee and a butter roll across the street. They know me there. When I finish that, I go into the park and lay back to sleep for a few hours so I feel it digest. When I wake up, I go and get me a beer. When I finish that, I go over to Trinity Church and get me an afternoon meal. If you homeless in New York, you shouldn't be hungry. There's a whole lot of places you can go to eat, even on the weekends they got kitchens all over the place. Trinity you can get a plate on Sunday at twelve o'clock. They let you eat at eleven if you went to church, but me, I wait to twelve. See, I can't go to services at Trinity, 'cause they Baptist. I'm Pentecostal, FIRM believer in Pentecostal churches. I know we all serve one God, but I believe in dancing of the spirit—talking in tongues. Baptists don't do that.

When I'm done eating lunch, I go on the avenue and make a little change. I used to get a Social Services check when I first got out here, but now I have to make all my money panhandling. I don't mind it so much. It's important to be polite and say hello to the people. I like putting smiles on people's faces, so I make a lot of little jokes. Like if they have a little dog, I might say, "Fifi is that you?" People crack up. Depending on how busy the street is, it might take a few hours to get enough money for some beer. I never lose my patience, and I understand when people can't give. After I get my money for two or three forties, I chill out in the park for the rest of the day.

At night, I've got a crew of brothers that I sleep with. We look out for each other. What one has, everybody has. It's not just you have, everybody has. When you go to bed, one stays up until he gets tired, and then he wakes up the next guy, and he goes to sleep. You watch over the rest. All together there's probably about twenty people that I can trust. That over there—that's Vinny the Chimp, Bear, and Radio Rahim. That's Cool. We sleep right on 7 and A. It only tends to get a little rough on the weekends. Why? You got young folk that drink and don't know how to act.

You've gotta understand, I'm not out here because I HAVE to be. I'm out here because I WANT to be. It's not so much me being an alcoholic. I just like to drink. Things wasn't happening like I wanted, so I started drinking. Alcohol is not bad as long as you don't abuse it. If you abuse alcohol, that's where you start messing up. If you drink constantly and stop eating, your body starts deteriorating. You start to get sick. That's why I drink a lot of beer and very little alcohol. To me, certain beers are refreshing. I started off on beer, I guess I'll end up with beer.

I know that I've gotta do a better job taking care of myself. I'm thinking of going into Bellevue Men's Shelter when it get cold, but for right now, I'm just gonna be staying out here. Overall, I'm pretty happy. God has blessed me with a great life. I don't worry about what's gonna happen when I'm gone. They're just gonna take my ashes down to Coney Island and throw them in the ocean. I think the good Lord will take me.

As Phillip finishes the rest of his beer, he reaches up to wipe the stream of tears from his face.

Phillip disappears for a week in mid September. When he returns, he tells me that his brother had brought word that his mother had passed away, and he returned to the Rockaways to visit family. During his visit Janet bought him a Greyhound Bus ticket to stay with relatives in Louisiana for the winter.

I last spoke to Phillip on October 19th. He told me that he planed to return to New York in the spring of 2002. I have not seen him since.

Sweet Leif

Brooklyn, New York 1966

How are you gonna tell me that I didn't bring you your fucking booze? You gave me the money, I went to the fucking liquor store, and five minutes ago I put it right next to you right on the fucking bench. You're so fucking drunk you probably put it in your pocket and don't remember. Oh, I'm fulla shit? I'm fulla shit? Don't fuck with me Phillip! I'LL BASH YOU OVER THE HEAD WITH THIS FUCKING GARBAGE CAN!!!

Sweet Leif is an emotionally intense individual. Her small stature stands in stark contrast to her immense persona. She describes herself as a "no bullshit" person and never hesitates to share her viewpoints regardless of how they might be received. This headstrong attitude gains her respect but also creates many conflicts. I have seen her engage in several physical confrontations.

Witnessing Sweet Leif's vicious wrath makes me very apprehensive about asking for an interview. I finally approach her early one morning in July, and she is perfectly cordial. We walk to a secluded area of the park and embark on a marathon three-hour session. Although it is a humid eighty degrees, Sweet Leif is shivering. She rambles her responses in raspy spurts of epic proportion.

Our first apartment was in Bushwick, Brooklyn. I lived with my two younger brothers, my parents, and my grandparents. My dad used to work for the American Stock Exchange, and my mom was a housewife. After my grandfather died, we moved into an apartment house on Pitt Street in the Lower East Side. Now they're projects, but back then they were tenements.

On the outside we looked like a typical family, but behind closed doors it was a different story. My father was a drinker. He DRANK. My mom didn't have the guts to stand up to him, and she just got the shit kicked out of her. She would never tell my dad when we got in trouble, because he'd knock the shit out of us. I'm the oldest, so when he'd hit my younger brother, I'd wind up jumping in and taking the beating. I'd do the same for my mom. I didn't mind the fights that much, but what really hurt me was having to listen to my father tell me how worthless I was all the time.

My parents sent me to this bullshit Catholic school down the street for kindergarten. The only thing I remember is that stupid play we did, the fucking *Chicken Littles*. You know, where the sky is falling? I played a flower. I didn't wanna do it, because I had stage fright. They made me get up there in this stupid fucking cardboard costume, and I hated it.

That school drove me nuts. Whenever I came home my knuckles were always bright red from getting smacked with a ruler. In fourth grade I got caught smoking cigarettes outside, and I told Sister Agatha to go to hell. Poor nun almost had a heart attack. Finally I got kicked out of Catholic school. My father was pissed. I don't know why. He's an atheist.

I went to a public middle school, but it really didn't make a difference. I didn't want to be in school, period. I was a little bit unsure of myself, and the kids picked on me a lot.

I used to have a big crush on one of the guys in my class. He was always disruptive all the time. I guess I liked him, because I thought he was a badass. One day he asked me to meet him at the pizza shop, so I got all dressed up in a nice dress, and I waited for him for like an hour. He showed up with a bunch of other girls, and he started making fun of me, telling me I was ugly and shit. I didn't want to go back to school after that, but my mother made me.

I remember in seventh grade there was this other girl who they used to pick on, Luan. She really was ugly—nerdy glasses, afro red hair and freckles all over her face. She liked this guy named Mark. He thought he was god's gift to women, a real player. He took Luan out for pizza one night and told her he wanted to have sex. Luan went and told all the popular girls, and they said she should do it. But really, they were just setting her up. See, all the popular girls were talking about how they had sex, but they were actually virgins.

That night, Mark brought Luan to a keg party in Forest Park. I saw them walking away up into the woods, and Mark turned around and gave one of his friends the thumbs-up sign. After a few minutes, this group of guys started following. Mark was up there fucking away with Luan, and his friends came up and shined this huge flashlight on them. Luan started crying and told Mark to stop, but he just started laughing and kept fucking her. Pretty much, at that point, it turned into rape. That fucked up Luan pretty bad. We didn't see her in school after that.

My father lost his job when I was eleven, and we wound up losing a lot of stuff and going into debt. Eventually, he declared bankruptcy and became a building contractor. He went from making seventy-five thousand a year to thirty thousand. Kids in school would call me a welfare kid, because I was always wearing secondhand clothes. I was very self-conscious. Kids used to beat me up every day for no fucking reason, just for GP, general purpose.

I was a real terror to all of my teachers, always yelling or throwing stuff around the classroom. I figured that if I started causing trouble, the teachers would at least start having to listen to me. They tried to ignore me, but that only made me get more frustrated.

By the time I got to high school things at home were really out of control with my father. When I was thirteen, we had a big argument. He was smacking me around, and he told me, "If you don't like it, you can get the fuck out." I wasn't going to back down, so I ran away from home.

I didn't really have anywhere to go, so I went to Tompkins Square. I was just sitting on the street, and this old guy asked me what I was doing. I told him my story, and he said that I could sleep inside his tent in the park for the night.

At first I was a little bit scared to be sleeping in the park, but everybody was really friendly. They saw that I was just a little girl, and they looked out for me, because they didn't want to see me get raped. It was like a family. Eventually the cops took me home, but I always ended up back here in the park for days at a time.

I used to sleep in a tent right over by that tree over there. That was where I made the transition from being the little girl that everybody picked on to somebody who didn't take any shit. It was also the place where I became an addict. About the third time that I slept here, I was in a tent with a junkie, he's dead now God rest his soul, and I asked him to explain what he was doing. I was curious about what it was like, and I told him that I wanted to try it one time. He said, "You never try this stuff just one time. I've been doing it every day for thirty-five years."

I kept on asking him, and eventually he gave in. He mainlined me a little bit, and bam. It was like the best orgasm that you've ever had in your life. Everything just melted. It lasted for like four hours. I fell in love. For the next seventeen years, I kept trying to get that first time rush. It never happened.

That year was pretty rough. In the fall my boyfriend of two years got killed in a car crash. My grandmother died right after.* I couldn't deal with it, so I ended up coming down to Tompkins Square to shoot up a lot. Within a month or so I had to shoot up about four times a day. The cost wasn't anything like what it is today, they used to sell huge bags right on 2nd Street for three dollars. I used to go to school and snort during lunch. Then I'd do a bag at night, but I'd

---

*Sweet Leif's name came from the "tender healing herbs" in her grandmother's garden.

always make sure that I had some left for the morning. It was pretty easy to hide what I was doing, and it
actually made me a lot calmer.

When I was sixteen, I dated this guy Roger who I
later found out was a pimp. We both needed money
for our habits, so he conned me into going out on the
stroll. I'd get twenty bucks for giving head. I was so
emotionally messed up that it didn't really faze me. It
was mechanical. It didn't matter. I made decent
money, but Roger would take most of it.

One thing about being a prostitute was that I
totally lost my attraction for men. Looking back on all
the fucked up shit that men had done to me, it's no
wonder that I became a lesbian. Today I'm totally gay
and I love it.

After a few months of working the streets, I fell in
love with this girl named June who was a dominatrix.
She brought me over to Hellfire and got me a job
there. Instead of doing sex, I was doing dominance. I
was making more money, and I didn't even have to
fuck.

I stayed with June for a while, but eventually we
went our separate ways, and I ended up sleeping in
the park. Tompkins was different back then, everybody knew everybody, and people looked out for each
other. Sometimes the meat market on 14th Street
would give us free steaks, and we'd barbecue right on
top of the garbage cans. One time they came home
with a whole side of beef. Even the cops used to say
hello. A lot of the old time cops were really cool.
Captain Kelly and Captain Dunn used to stop by and
give us money or a doggie bag.

There never used to be many cops in Tompkins.
It was mostly park rangers. It wasn't a police state like

it is now. As long as you weren't mugging anybody, you could drink, smoke a joint, shoot up, or whatever. There were a lot of hippies and black people, but mostly old-time junkies—guys who were shooting dope for forty years.

I was still doing a lot of dope, and I had to start selling to support my habit. My dealer used to pay me in dope. For every six bags I sold, I got four bags for myself. I used to move eight bundles of ten bags each every day. It wasn't too hard, because I knew everybody. I would hit the front gate and I'd have twenty people running up to me.

The park was wild. The men's room used to be the heroin cop spot, and the ladies' room was the brothel. This lady had a mattress in the back stall, and johns would pay her at the door. She's dead now. Somebody gave her a hot shot of battery acid, because she was ripping people off and ratting people out.

For the most part the people in the park were pretty peaceful. Whenever there was fights, it was always caused by somebody who didn't live here. One time this guy from New Jersey tried to take over my tent. I went and got a few of the boys, and they grabbed him and threw him over the fence. "If you come back into this park, we'll kill you." The people in the park today don't have that sense of unity. Today, they'll slit your throat for a dollar.

I was away from Tompkins Square for the first riot, but I was there for the second one in 1991. It was a sunny day, and there was going to be a punk show in the bandshell called *Resist to Exist*. Before the show could get started, the bands had to wait for the representative of the Parks Department to get there. He was stuck in traffic, and he was a half hour late. When he finally got there, he told the bands that they could play for an extra half hour. So the concert went on, and everyone was having a good time. Apparently, the police hadn't spoken with the Parks Commissioner, so they expected the concert to be over a half hour earlier. When the time on the permit ran out, the cops went up on stage and pulled the plug. The commissioner went over to talk to the cops, but they pushed him off the stage. Then total chaos broke out.

Cops were pushing everybody off the stage and throwing instruments. Then the crowd started throwing stuff at the cops. They went berserk and started knocking everybody with riot clubs—even the people who were trying to get away. I got hit with a nightstick behind my ear.

I ran out to Avenue A where a bunch of my friends started dragging boxes and chairs into the middle of the street . There was like thirty horses coming down St. Marks, and people were just getting squashed. Somebody tossed me a can of lighter fluid and I squirted it on the pile. The cops saw what we were doing, and they took me down and handcuffed me. They beat the fuck out of me and cracked my ribs. Just as I was riding away in the car, I saw the flames shoot up.

After the riots, they put up a twenty-foot fence around the park, and nobody could get in. When it reopened, they closed the park at midnight, and that was the end of Tent City. Some of the people from those days are still around. A few of them got their act together. A lot of them died.

As the summer sun climbs higher, Sweet Leif's trembling increases. When we finish our second tape, I give her the agreed upon sum of twenty dollars even though I know what she's going to do with it.

I speak to Sweet Leif several times in the next few months. In August she is arrested for drunk and disorderly conduct and is sentenced to three days community service cleaning up the park. Some of the regulars taunt her by intentionally leaving garbage in areas she has just finished cleaning. The ensuing outbursts are a source of much amusement for the bench dwellers. I finally get the chance to speak to Sweet Leif again towards the end of September.

After Tent City died, the heroin started getting more expensive. A lot of the old time dealers got arrested, and it was hard to find somebody you could trust. In '95 they had some kids up on St. Marks selling rat poison saying, "Ha Ha fuck these junkies." They'd take a bundle and have eight bags of dope and two bags of strychnine. It was like Russian roulette. Twenty-eight people died and nineteen were put in the hospital. Those kids are in jail for murder now. My younger brother died from that. That hit me pretty hard. The night I found out, some guy was bad-mouthing my brother, and I just exploded. We got into a fistfight, and he sliced my face. That's how I got this scar.

In '96 one of the store owners on Avenue A thought I was stealing his newspapers, and he called the cops. I didn't steal nothing, but the police searched me and found a gun.

I quit heroin cold turkey in the holding cells. For five days before my court date, I just sweat it out. It's the hardest thing I've ever had to do. You're shitting and puking at the same time. Anything you eat comes right up. Every joint and bone in your body aches.

You can't sleep. You're sweating one moment, and you're freezing the next. It could be ninety degrees, and you'd be shivering. It's just like if you don't get food, you get hungry. If your body's used to having dope, it expects to be fed.

I was in jail for eight months, and then I went to a treatment center for nine months. It was full of shit. They weren't allowing me to advance. The worst thing about it was the encounter groups. You sat in a chair called the hot seat, and everybody nit picked what they didn't like about you. Then, they'd tell you all the things that were going to make you get high. They didn't even know who I was. Fuck them. I used to hide in the landscaping room when it was time for group. Rehab is worse than jail. They don't get on your case in jail.

Once I got back on the street, I didn't have anywhere to go, so I moved in with my mother in Long Island. I started working some different jobs, and I stayed clean. The last time I had a job was October of 2000. I was working as a bar back in the East Village. They fired me because they thought I robbed the register.

After that I started camping out around Tompkins Square again. My mother still has a lot of my stuff in Long Island, and she feeds my cat. Last winter I moved into the women's shelter on 25th and Lexington. One night, I wasn't going to make it back by ten o'clock, so I called and told the receptionist. The next morning, my shit was packed and they already gave my bed away. I guess the receptionist never put it on the books. I couldn't find another spot. Since February, I've been sleeping out here.

A couple months ago, I started doing dope again.

At first it was just a little bit, and then I wouldn't touch it for a month. Now I'm doing it everyday. The heroin culture has changed a lot since the old days. The people now are more selfish. The attitude of the seller has changed. It's all about a quick buck, and I don't care if you're sick. Half the time, it's not even dope. They're putting baking soda in there. The dealers are ripping people off, because most of them are kids who don't even get high.

The people who hang out in the park annoy me to no end. I walked in the other day, and Phillip says, "Kinda late Sweet Lips. I might have to spank your little behind." I think Phillip has a crush on me. I told him straight up that I'm not giving him no play. You know I'm gay, but on top of that if I'm going to go back to a man, I'm definitely not going to sleep with a fifty something homeless man who stinks. He's not a bad guy, but he pisses me off. He tells me that I'm cute when I'm mad, but I ain't going to be so fucking cute when I hit you over the head with a fucking garbage can. *(laughs)*

When I get my check, all the guys say buy me a beer. Give me a cigarette. Excuse me, when I applied for welfare, I do believe I was by myself, and I don't believe I claimed any dependents. You're too damn lazy to drag your ass to the welfare office to get a little pocket change for yourself. That's what pisses me off. They want to sit in this park all fucking day long, won't even go panhandle. They want to drink up everybody's beer and have their food brought to them on a silver platter. They won't even get off their lazy ass to go to the goddamned bathroom.

The whole World Trade Center thing is fucking me up. My younger brother got blown up. My mom's not taking that too easy. I was sitting there on 7th Street, and I heard this big boom. We thought it was Con Ed releasing pressure from the boilers. I went up to my friend Joe's roof, and we saw the second plane hit. I just started walking downtown with my friend Froggy. We were about three blocks away when it went down. There was this big fucking fireball that shot out, and we just ran under this ramp in this construction site. We saw people jumping off the buildings. I'm still kind of fucked up about that.

Sweet Leif disappears from the park in October. I finally spot her walking down Avenue A in early December, and we step into Odessa's Restaurant to go over her rough draft. She tells me that she has kicked heroin and is living with friends in Long Island. With great pride she shows me a roll of pictures that she had shot while working as a volunteer at Ground Zero.

The Chess Monster

New York, New York 1951

Most people come into this park, and they want to play the same old game of chess with the pieces set up the same old way. They want to bang on the clock and memorize what they need to do to win. In Chess Monster Chess, each game has it's own individual character. You can't use somebody else's strategy, because you have to be thinking in the moment. Some people don't want to play Chess Monster Chess, but that's OK, because someday it's going to revolutionize the way people play the game.

Between interviews in the Living Room, I spend many hours relaxing at the chess tables. Chess Monster and I play several times during the summer and fall. He is well kept and always sober. I don't begin to suspect that he's homeless until I find him in the Second Avenue subway station during the winter. We have our first real conversation in January when I invite Chess to keep me company on the ride back to my apartment in Bensonhurst.

Once we grab a seat on the F train, he pulls a scrapbook from his bag and removes an old clipping from the New York Post *that shows him in his Chess Monster costume. He then removes a small packet of papers titled "Chess Monster Chess." With great pride he pages through and explains the rules for his creation. Basically, Chess Monster Chess is the same as regular chess, except the players can arrange the back row of pieces anyway they want. Chess explains the particulars of castling and en passant with great relish, but when I try to steer the conversation away from chess, his words slow to a trickle. When I begin to ask him personal questions, he replies that it's "classified information."*

As I become more familiar with Chess, he reveals that his real name is Lewis. In spring of 2002 he agrees to talk about his life.

I grew up in Whitechester—I mean Westchester. The racial thing was very subtle, because I didn't fit in with the so-called typical blacks. I always kind of resented it when white people told me, "Oh you're one of the good Negroes. You're not like the others." It was kind of hard having to associate with two groups, because a lot of the black people would say, "Look at him he's trying to be white."

My father died in January of 1968, and then that April Martin Luther King was assassinated. The first thing that came out of my mother's mouth was that they had to do something for the natural leaders in the black community like myself. They needed to give us something to hold on to, or we would be the ones leading the riots. That June I was one of two hundred black kids to get a full ride to NYU.

After I graduated, I worked as a history teacher for a year, but back then there was a teacher surplus, so I had to go to work for All State Insurance. I hated it. When the company relocated, I quit.

In 1976 Jimmy Carter had something called the CETA *(Comprehensive Employment Training Act)*. It was basically a make work program that was supposed to keep everybody happy. They gave you jobs as janitors and security guards. Now I had a college degree, so that was way beneath me, but the pay was like a thousand dollars a month, about the same as I would have been making teaching.

I went down to the unemployment office, and the guy down there talked me into it. Being a college graduate, I didn't really fit the profile for the program, but they had to have all the jobs filled, or they'd lose their funding. It was all right. For the first few months I helped guys repair buildings in New Rochelle. Then I got a job as a janitor in a nursing home. I didn't really work too hard.

There I was with a college degree, and in theory they were getting me ready for future employment. I knew there wasn't any future in it, but the benefits were great, and I had a lot of free time. That's when I started coming down to the city to play chess.

The thing that always appealed to me about chess was that there were almost an infinite number of games that could be played. It blew my mind just to ponder the complexity. I said why not take the potential for different possibilities and expand on that. I discovered that instead of setting up the pieces the same way every time, if you changed the order in the back row, the game had so many more strategic possibilities.

That was the birth of Chess Monster Chess. In

order to promote my new game, I put together this
costume made out of giant chess pieces and a motorcycle helmet. I used to wear it down to the park.

While I was down here, I met this guy, Jerry, who
had a costume place in the Bronx. He said that he
wanted me to be a guest monster at a monster con-
vention that they were having at Madison Hotel.
There were seven hundred people in the auditorium
and all sorts of different monsters. *Chess's voice begins to
tremble.* Jim, I went into that auditorium and complete
strangers were taking my picture. People were asking

for my autograph. I was kissing babies. It was like a rush, a high. Right after that, a reporter came down to the park and gave me a one-page write up in the *New York Post*. It was like I found my calling. I quit my job, and from that moment I knew that I wanted to be the Chess Monster for the rest of my life.

My family thought I was crazy when I started turning into the Chess Monster. There was a thread of anger through it. "Boy you better use that college degree. Go work for the system." I guess I could have bought myself a three-piece suit and gone for some interviews, but I just didn't see the point. My experience working for All State was completely empty. I knew that any other job I got would be the same thing. After a while, I stopped going back home to my mom's house in Westchester.

Remember the singer Barbara Streisand? Her parents told her that she should be an airline stewardess. Bill Cosby's dad told him he'd never make it as a comedian. That keeps me inspired to be the Chess Monster.

I've got cousins around here that I stay with most of the time. Other times I stay outside, but I don't worry about it, because as long as I've got my chessboard, I don't need to worry about anything else. I know that I'm a little bit of a sociopath, but I don't think I'm any crazier than most people in this city. A lot of these people are running around working nine-to-five, and they don't even know what they want from life. I know what I want from life. I want to be the Chess Monster.

I continue to play with Chess Monster in the park. He tells me that he's currently seeking a patent for his creation.

Jerome

New York, New York 1961

I first meet Jerome when he asks me for a dollar in the middle of the park. Dressed in a button down shirt and neatly creased slacks, he certainly doesn't look like he's sleeping on the street. Not wanting to waste my resources on an unlikely subject for an interview, I reach into my pocket and give him a dime. He thanks me cheerfully, and I continue on my way.

I circle around the park one more time in search of a more credible subject. When no opportunities arise, I return to Jerome. After an awkward interchange, I find out that he is in fact homeless. Jerome responds with rapid-fire clarity spewing thick mentholated clouds.

My mother is a touchy subject. I didn't get to meet her until I was thirteen years old. All that I knew was that she gave birth to me in Harlem Hospital. My grandmother didn't want to see us get separated in the foster care system, so she went to court and gained custody of me and my brothers and sisters. I didn't have any resentment toward my real mother, but I used to hear a lot of stories about why she didn't want us.

Grandma had her own house. It wasn't an apartment. Back in the forties she used to do domestic work for this man named Samuel Greene, a banker somewhere out in Long Island. They had a good relationship, and he was very good to her in his will, so she bought a nice two-family in Brighton Beach.

I have eight sisters and seven brothers, but only three of us are actually from the same mother and father. There were four of us living with our grandmother, and we all had our own bedrooms. My brother Robert and I were best friends. He was only a year older than me, and we did everything together, sports, movies, mischief. I was his little showpiece. We were really close. My father was working as a truck driver, and he used to keep his stuff there, but mostly he was out on the road.

I pretty much had everything I could want as a kid. When Christmas or birthdays would come around we were always provided for. Allowance, naturally I had to earn that by keeping my grades up and doing chores. I was very independent. When I was thirteen, I was always going to Pathmark and packing bags to generate my own income. I got passing grades and played sports. I had my friends, and I had a beautiful girlfriend. Things were great, but that all changed in 1976.

One day my sister came home and told my older brothers that this boy in the neighborhood raped her. It was date rape, somebody she knew. The next day, I was walking down the street on my way home from school, and I ran into my brothers. They had found the guy, and they were working themselves into a tizzy. Something just clicked inside when I saw him. It was like there was an outside force. I wasn't even controlling what I was doing.

I ran to the house and went upstairs to my father's room and opened up his chest and got his .22 pistol, then I ran down to where my brothers were at, and I shot this guy in the chest. Everything was in slow motion, like I was in a trance. I could hear, but it was like everything was far, far away from me. I could hear my brothers yelling, "What did you do? What did you do? Come on! We gotta get out a here!" I don't remember anything after that. He died en route to the hospital. I can't say that I intended to kill him, but that's the end result.

I went to school the next day in a daze. Two days later the homicide detectives came to the house to arrest me. My brother Phillip tried to take the weight, because I was the youngest, but the cops knew that it was me. Right after they took me away, my grandmother had a heart attack. By the grace of God it wasn't fatal. When she came out of the hospital, she sold the house to try to post my bail. As soon as she did that, they raised bail from a quarter million to a half million. I had to spend the duration of the pretrial period in C74ARDC (*Adolescent Reformatory Detention Center*) on Riker's Island.

Judge Horace Billings denied the motion to have me tried as a juvenile. Most of the testimony came from police. They didn't even have the actual gun. They got a different gun from out of nowhere. The trial went on for weeks. In the end, twelve respected jurors found me guilty of murder in the first degree. It's hard to find the words to describe that feeling. When the judge read the sentence of twenty-five years to life, I fell into shock and had to be revived.

I made my rounds through the prison system, Attica, Clinton, Dannemora, Sing Sing. There are some differences, but the procedures are the same. I got my GED in prison, then I went on to get an associates degree. At the time Mario Cuomo had something called the Pell program that provided money for secondary education. I tried to make my situation as bearable as I could. I wrote a lot of letters to my family and my girlfriend. They were there for me, and that gave me the strength to maintain. My grandmother was always making money moves on the outside to get me an appeal.

Prison toughens you up. You'll do things that you

could never imagine yourself doing for survival pur-
poses. The corruption at the administrative level
makes you resentful. Guards allow fucked-up shit to
happen as a means to controlling the population. If a
guard has a problem with a certain prisoner, he'll look
the other way if he's attacked.

The worst experience that I had was in Clinton.
That's way upstate, almost eleven hours from the city.
There's no black officers there. None. Everybody is
what we call rednecks—no disrespect. They certainly
had no problem letting me know that I was a nigger.
When you come in they say, "Listen nigger! We'll kill
you and write your people and say you got transferred, but if you do what you're supposed to do,
you'll get out alive."

One of the only things that I looked forward to
was talking to this Christian lady who used to visit with
the prisoners. She would bring us packages, and
maybe talk about the Word. We had a pretty good
relationship. It wasn't anything inappropriate, but she
used to hug me when she said good-bye. One of the
guards named Miller just stared me down. You could
just see the hatred all over his eyes. He said, "Oh, so
you like to grope and fondle white women. How would
you like it if someone groped and fondled you?"

I took what the officer said lightly. Then one day
my cell cracked at 10:30 at night. That was unusual,
because it was lights out. One of the guards told me
that I had a tier hearing. That didn't make sense,
because I hadn't received any misbehavior reports. I
didn't want to get in any trouble, so I obeyed the com-
mand and walked down to the hearing office. All the
lights were out, so I walked over to the Sergeants
office. When I opened the door I saw Miller in there

with three other inmates.

They raped me in front of him.

You're the first person I've ever told that story to. I certainly didn't tell my family. I went crazy after that. I had to be put in a separate cell and nobody could go near me. When I finally got my senses back, I found one of the prisoners who had violated me, and I stabbed him with a homemade knife. I received another charge for that, but I really didn't care. I figured that I'd never be a free man anyway. Eventually they dropped that charge because it was a retaliatory act.

In 1981 I was given a gift from God. I received a notification from my attorney that my appeal was going to be heard. It was on the grounds that Judge Billings made an error trying me as an adult. That letter was like an angel had put his hands on me. I never thought that I'd ever experience freedom again. It took three years for the appeal to be processed. Then they re-sentenced me for five to fifteen. It took another two years for me to finally get out. I made my first parole board on June 21, 1986.

That was a beautiful day. I literally dropped down on the ground and kissed it. After spending ten years in a fucking cage amongst the horrors of that life, that was total euphoria, like I was able to fly. Unbelievable. But even though I was in ecstasy at that moment, I was still bitter. I maintain that cynicism to this day. A few days ago I had a confrontation with an officer at the entrance of the park. One of my friends told me that I should know better, but I have absolutely no respect for the law. The purpose of the penal system isn't to rehabilitate. It's there to punish. Nobody is normal after surviving incarceration.

I moved in with my girlfriend when I got home.

We got married three months later. She worked for the Department of Human Services, and I used the vocational skills that I picked up in jail to get me a construction job as a framer and welder. I was bringing home close to eleven hundred dollars every two weeks with overtime.

At that point it was crazy for me to consider doing anything illegal. But when I was on the inside, I was hearing all about the riches that you could make with just a little bit of rock. When I came out I actually saw it. All the guys who were younger than me were driving Mercedes and wearing diamonds. I just couldn't resist the temptation.

For four years I had a lucrative run in selling large quantities of cocaine. I was never a street peddler, and I never really used my product except once in a while. I was certainly the man. I had three drug houses and was making ten thousand dollars a week. I bought a brand new BMW 325I and a Jeep Grand Cherokee. My father was a Buick man, so I bought him a new car for father's day in 1988. I used to be so flush that if I was sitting on the toilet and there was no toilet paper I would pull out a ten-dollar bill and wipe my ass.* It also felt good to hook up my grandmother. I used to hit her with five hundred dollars cash and send her on cruises. She didn't know how I was getting it, but I think she suspected.

In 1990 I started moving my operations into more affluent, white areas. You see, anywhere you put drugs, the fabric of the community starts to deteriorate. People become addicted and they do whatever they have to do to get that money. It's one thing to sell drugs in the ghetto. It's another to do it in a

---

*Upon reviewing the draft, Jerome told me to change the ten to a fifty.

wealthy area. I was driving my Jeep Cherokee through the Upper West Side with five thousand dollars in my pocket, and DEA agents pulled me over and searched my vehicle. They asked me where I got the money from, and I gave them a smart-ass answer. I said, "I'm in the Christian Coalition and I just finished taking up a collection."

The agent smacked me in the face and said, "Smart nigger get your hands up. I'll blow your fucking head off." I posted $150,000 bail and hired an excellent attorney. The quality of my attorney was what allowed me to get the minimum sentence of seven years. In '93 they took away my house and my car, and I went back upstate.

My day-to-day existence flowed a bit more smoothly than my first incarceration. I knew about the ins an outs of penitentiary life. I got involved in a lot of little hustles that allowed me to get my cigarettes. One bad thing was that Pataki killed the Pell program, so I couldn't go for a bachelor's degree.

After I'd been locked up for a while, my wife started acting real strange. It seemed like something was eating on her, and she didn't know how to come out and tell me. On top of that every time that I used to call, my brother Robert would pick up the phone. At first I didn't think anything of it, but then it started happening every time I called. I'd ask him for my wife, and he'd make excuses for her not coming to the phone. He gave me this that and the third. One day I just came out and asked him straight up. I told him, "No matter what you say, you're my brother, nothing's gonna change that." I had to put him at ease by telling him that. Then I straight out asked him to be forthright. "Are you fucking my wife?" He didn't answer me immediately. He said that he wanted to write me a letter to explain. I said that there was no need for that. I just hung up the phone.

My wife is as much to blame, but the fact that Robert was my brother makes him more responsible. A woman is going to be a woman, but my brother should have known how it would devastate me. That put a wedge in our relationship. I haven't seen him since my grandmother died in 1996. My behavior was good, so they let me go to the wake. I saw my brother, and I hugged him, but we didn't speak. That wasn't the time and place for that. I went and sat in a pew away from everybody else and mourned. I haven't spoken to him since then.

Once I got out of jail, I ended up out on the streets. I still have family, and I don't have to be out here, but once my grandmother passed, it seemed like everybody just split up and went their own way. I'm in touch with my sisters, but at no time do they invite me to come over. I have too much pride to ask for help.

My wife and I are still legally married. She's willing to get back with me, but I don't want that. See, I can't take the chance of being with her, because if she cheats on me I'll literally kill her. You know why? When you kill once it becomes easy.

Right now, I'm going to Kingsboro Shelter. I'm not really comfortable going there, because it reminds me too much of prison. They give you a HA *(Housing Authority)* number, and I can't deal with that number mindset. I might shower there once in a while, but lately I sleep outside in the East Village. This is where I hung out back in the late eighties when times were flush. I'm in a much lower situation now, but I still have friends in the area, and it's good to see them.

I'm just trying to soul search. I need time to think. I certainly don't want to be involved in crime or the drug trade anymore. If I add up all of the years that have been taken out of my life, I see that it's not worth it. Don't get me wrong. I want money, but this time I want it the right way. I hate being in the streets, but my pride won't allow me to go to my family and ask them for help. Especially being forty, I don't even know how to do that.

I'm going to start a job doing some construction on 9th Street next week. Hopefully they'll be pleased with my performance and keep me on. Then maybe I can find a furnished room and save some money. I obviously don't have a relationship now. That's not something I have to deal with. The focus is me. I don't want a relationship built on what a person can do for me. I like to be able to bring something to the table. Even when people appear to be generous, if you don't offer them something in return, it takes a toll on them. I'm just trying to put myself into a situation where I can stand on my own two feet.

It is two weeks before I talk to Jerome again. His clean clothes are gone, and he has a dew rag covering his head. I wouldn't have recognized him if he didn't call out my name. His cheery composure is replaced by an apprehensive twitching, and his confident voice now trembles in tentative restraint. He reads the first draft of his interview in a discombobulated but projecting tone for a puzzled audience of old Ukrainian women. He becomes irate at several minor inconsistencies and is furious that I had given his brother an alias. Before he can complete the reading, he asks me for five dollars to get some Chinese food. I have not seen him since.

Vinny
New York, New York 1941

*Vinny is a solitary soul. He can often be found sitting
alone, rigid as a board, sipping a beer while reading through
old newspapers. At night he lies down with Phillip's group of
old timers on 7th Street. At first Vinny is very reluctant to let me
record him, but after we get to know each other, he finally agrees
to project his gritty New York tones into my tape recorder.*

My grandparents came over from Ireland and
Germany, and my mother and father grew up in the
Bronx and Manhattan. We lived in a railroad flat
right on 3rd Avenue right above Thirty-third.
Remember that old song? I'm on the East Side at
Thirty-third and Third? *(hums a faint melody)*

Believe it or not, there was seventeen of us. I'm
the seventeenth. It was a heavy apartment. I'll tell you
that. Two or three of us had to sleep in one bed. The
girls had one of the side rooms and my father and

mother had the other side room. My uncle Joey slept in the kitchen by the bathtub. There was a homemade shower that we hooked up over the tub, and the toilet was down the hall.

My mother worked and my father worked. My older brothers and sisters worked. Everybody had to give some money to help with the rent. Back then my parents were paying twenty-eight sixty a month for six rooms. It was cheaper, because it was a cold-water flat. You had to get hot water from a belly stove. Was it cold in the winter? Like you wouldn't believe. When they outlawed the belly stoves we had to use a gas stove. Then they outlawed that in '57 and put in a boiler for steam heat. After that, the rent went sky high. It went from twenty-eight dollars to sixty-eight dollars. When my mother and father died in the early seventies, we left the apartment. Today they're charging three thousand dollars a month.

My father would wake up at five o'clock every morning and go down to Cushman's Bakery and get some rolls. He left at quarter to six to drive a truck for Schaffer's Brewery. Every stop that he made was a bar. They'd all say, "Hey Willie! Have a drink!" Every night when he came home, he was cockeyed as a fiddle, always sauced. My mother used to hit him with a frying pan. He'd be hung over in the morning, but he always went to work on time. He never touched booze, but he could handle his beer.

My father was real big on discipline. If you did something wrong, you were punished severely. He made you put your hands out like this, and he'd hit you with this hickory rod. If you flinched, you got it worse. We always used to have to go from school right home to the house. Sometimes we'd try to sneak out and visit

our friends when we were taking out the garbage. My
mom was soft, but when my father got home he'd say,
"You know the procedure." That's the exact thing he
used to say. WHAP! It hurt like a bandit. Sometimes
he'd tell you to lay down on the bathtub cover and he'd
whip yah in the ass with a garrison belt. Goddamn that
would hurt, but I'd hold the tears in. I heard my father
say to my mother once, "Janet I don't wanna hit him,
but he just won't cry. If he cried I'd stop."

My neighborhood was Irish, German, Italians,
and Greeks. We got along pretty good. When the
Hispanics first started coming, we kept our distance.
After a while we learned to live with each other, but it
wasn't like I could have brought a Puerto Rican girl
home. See, my father was from the old, old, old,
school. Two of my sisters married Italians, and my
father blew his stack. There was always that little gap
in the nationalities.

Black people didn't start coming down into
Midtown until the seventies. Years ago, 125th Street
was the borderline. You didn't go up there. They did-
n't come down here. Sometimes during the week we
mingled, but you didn't hang out up there. All the
Jews were down in the Lower East Side. We used to
say, "We're going down to Jewtown to get our suits for
Easter." But now it's all intermingled.

We went to church every Sunday at nine o'clock
at Sacred Heart on Second Avenue. That was the
biggest thing. I always fell asleep. I didn't understand
a word, because everything was in Latin. I used to go
blah, blah, blah, blah. What did I know? I went to
public school.

I went to P.S. 116 for grade school. It was tough,
but it made me smart. Teachers then were teachers.

When they taught you, they taught you. They used to call your house if you weren't doing your homework. In them days that's how close your family was to the school. When you got home, you better have a pad on your ass underneath your pants. *(laughs)*

I went to a vocational high school in Chelsea for radio technology. Then after school I'd go to work. It was easy to find work back then, not like it is today. You could work in a butcher store, or Macy's, or Gimble's as a stock boy. I mostly stocked shelves in the grocery store on the corner. I made fifteen dollars a week working five to nine. I had to be home at nine thirty. My sisters had to be home exactly at nine, because it was different for girls.

As I got older I started going out into the city by myself. It wasn't like it is today with the cops bothering you for drinking beer. I was pretty wild—one time we stole a car. It was great times. The biggest thing was hanging out in the ice cream parlor. I used to try to fazzle dazzle the girls. Be my girl, all this shit—pretty much try to get laid. That wasn't that easy back in those days. My father used to say to all of us boys, "If you knock up a girl, I'm making sure you're marrying her."

Sure enough I did.

I was seventeen, still in high school, and Maggie was fifteen. I met her at a dance at the Boys Club. She was a good girl, oh yeah. She didn't tell me that she got pregnant. She had her family tell my family. My dad could have ripped my head right outta my shoulders. He gave me two choices, go to jail or marry her. We got married in city hall. Both our families were there to make sure we did it. She was two months pregnant.

Nelson Hall

After the wedding, my father gave me two choices, go in the Navy, or go in the service. Fourteen days later, I was in Navy boot camp in the Great Lakes. They certified me as a radio repairman. When I got some leave, I went back to New York. From there, Maggie and I flew out to Hawaii. We got a nice two-room apartment. I was making a pretty solid chunk of change, but my check went to my wife. All I needed was pocket money.

After my wife gave birth to my son Vincent, she wanted to go back to New York to see her family. I only had a year left in Hawaii, so she took the baby back to New York. Once I got out of the service I went back to New York and we got a little apartment on 38th and 3rd.

We had one boy and four girls. For ten years I worked construction and unloading jobs. Then I started drinking a lot and fucking up. I'd spend my whole paycheck on booze. Maggie couldn't take it anymore, and one night she had the cops escort me out of the apartment. We separated after twelve years, but we never got a divorce. She's still my wife, married forty-five years. She moved out to Los Angeles four years ago with her mother and father and the kids. I haven't seen her since, but she still calls me every Christmas at my sister's house.

My son Vincent, he's a priest in the army. Two of my girls are married. My other girls are doing fine. Me, I started drinking even more, and in '86 I became a bum. I lost contact with my family except for my sister. I don't get my Navy pension. That goes to my wife for child support. I don't bother with GR. It's too much bullshit. I just panhandle to make my living.

I can't work because of my accident a year ago. I got drunk and broke my neck falling off a park bench. That was it. I was in Carbrini for a week. Then they transferred me to Bellevue and put a plate in the back of my neck. I had to stay there for eleven months. I can't turn my neck around, and my left side is numb. When I got out I ended up out here. You know the rest. My story is done. OK?

Vinny doesn't notice the black van cruising up on the Living Room. An officer steps out and points to the beer in his hand. "Vinny you got ID? Oh, did I interrupt your interview?"

No it's all right. *Vinny appears unfazed by the intrusion. He sorts through the contents of his baby stroller and pulls out a wrinkled piece of paper. Just as he is about to hand it to the officer, another call comes in over the radio and the officer has to leave. "Are you gonna be around later Vinny?"*

Yeah. I'll be around. *The police van rolls into the Eastern section of the park.* At least I get to finish my beer. That don't bother me much. Wasn't the first time, and it won't be the last time.

Vinny shows me the piece of paper, a list of his personal possessions from Riker's Island dated two weeks previous.

When I get seven tickets, they take me to Riker's for three days. After that, you get a clean sheet. It's all little bullshit. Once I get seven more slips, I'm going back to Riker's. *(laughs)* I'd say I've done the whole thing about three times. It's like paying taxes.

When the police return to give Vinny his ticket, they find him drinking another beer and issue him an extra ticket. I continue to visit with Vinny on a regular basis. Not much has changed.

Nancy Lane Smith

Buffalo, New York 1964

"Nancy's a real Hawthorne Wingo. That's a street term for somebody who gets along with everybody. You could walk past her, and then the next thing you know you're having a long conversation. You walk away feeling better about yourself and the people around you. You got the roughest cops out here, who don't like nobody, but they all love Nancy. You've got ambulance drivers who would tell everybody else to walk to the hospital. Not only will they take her to the hospital, but they'll bring her back here. She's a natural born Hawthorne Wingo." —Radio Rob

Nancy is an unfailingly affectionate individual. Each time I see her, she greets me with a peck on the cheek and a hug. Her jovial nature and willingness to laugh at herself endear her to the park regulars who refer to her affectionately as "Chicken Legs." Nancy has spent ten years around the park, and the regulars are her family. She often refers to people as "Uncle Rino," "Brother Gray Wolf" or "Sister Sweet Leif." The other bench dwellers take great pride in protecting their little sister. One night when an outsider ignites Nancy's temper, I watch six regulars rise from the bench and drive the man out of the park.

Nancy has many health issues. Cigarettes have reduced her voice to a hoarse whisper, and she has been hospitalized many times for acute fits of asthma combined with violent seizures. When these convulsions erupt, police officers and paramedics promptly file in from Avenue A to extract her in a stretcher. These emergencies happen so frequently that Nancy refers to the ambulances parked on the corner of St. Marks Place as "taxis." After one visit to Beth Israel in November, Nancy is sent to a three-day detox program. Within hours of her release, she is sitting in the park drinking malt liquor. Although Nancy carries an inhaler, she refuses to take certain medications for her seizures because of their violent reaction to alcohol.

Nancy and I talk almost every day. Although she is an extremely cooperative subject, her responses tend to be somewhat disjointed. This is particularly true after she has been drinking, when her normally affectionate nature sometimes shifts into a mercurial bitterness.

I was born in Buffalo, New York December 8th, 1964. My mother was drinking when she was pregnant, so I was an alcoholic baby. I never really knew my father, because he got shot coming out of a bar when I was just a baby. His name was Dunny Hill. He was a Cherokee. My mother's name is Lucille Smith. She was a Mohawk. I don't really remember too much about living with her, because she got paralyzed from the neck down in a car crash when I was two. After that, me and my sister went to live with my grandmother. Grandma used to take me to go visit my mother in the home. She always talked to us like little babies even when we were grown up. But I still respected her, so I wouldn't say nothing.

Sometimes my grandmother would take us to the Indian reservations. There were lots of cousins to play lacrosse and go swimming. The boys always used to tease me, and say that I was stupid. "So I'm stupid. I'll knock the living shit out of you!" I was always fighting a lot of boys. When I went to school, I always had a half-day, because I would punch somebody and get suspended. I wasn't very smart in school.

I remember I started smoking cigarettes when I was seven. I would steal my grandpa's Pall Malls, and the world would just go around in circles. *(laughs)* Everyday, I'd take one, and my grandma would give me a smack. But I love smoking cigarettes. There's nothing wrong with that. Even though I lost my voice the wrong way and my grandfather's dead from cancer—may he rest in peace.

When I was about twelve I used to take liquor from my grandma. I called it ice cream. When Grandma found out that I was drinking, she gave me an ass whooping left and right. We used to have a pretty big house, so I would run from one room to another. One time I hid in the chimney. When my aunt and uncle came in and found me, I started hitting them. I hit my aunt even though she's mental retarded. That was wrong—I know—I made a mistake. But why you gotta go tell grandma?

When I was thirteen I ran away. When the police found me, they put me in a group home on Allen Street in Buffalo.

I was raped.

Me and my girlfriend Sheila snuck out of the foster home and went over to this guy Joey's place in

Buffalo to smoke some reefer. I didn't want to smoke it, but I went to make sure that Sheila was all right. Everything was good, but when we were leaving all the sudden Joey snatched Sheila and threw her in the bedroom. I went and locked myself in the bathroom. I was in there for a while, and he was pounding on the door. I wouldn't open it. I said, "Let my friend alone!" Then I came out, because I wouldn't leave Sheila like that. He said, "Take off your clothes!"

I said, "Joey, Joey, why you gonna do this? You know me since I was a young kid. Don't you touch her! Don't you touch me!" But he did. He had a knife right there too. One of his friends came to the house. He told us to shut up, don't say a word. Sheila jumped up and was beating on them, and I was fighting the best I can, "You're not touching me fucking faggot motherfucker! I'm gonna tell your wife!" And—I didn't know what the fuck—I couldn't stop him. When he let us go, we got Sheila's mother. The cops went to Joey's house and saw the blood all over. *At this point in the interview Nancy is sobbing deeply. Radio Rob hands her a tissue to dry her face.*

I was scared. I talked to the cops, but I didn't want to go to court. Sheila and I already let everybody know what happened, so Joey went to jail. They didn't want me to stay in Buffalo, so Joey's wife sent me down to New York to be in foster care. Her name was Mary.

When I got off the bus in Manhattan, I saw all the busy trains, and I didn't understand. I didn't know where the hell I was. I got picked up by Carla. She was an Indian sister who was going to take me into a group home. I stayed with her for a week, then I ran away. I used to hang out on the streets and panhandle, then I'd take that money and buy beer.

You know the peep shows on 42nd Street? I used to work there doing live sex shows in a booth. I was fourteen. The first time was with a guy named Apache. I just keep my eyes closed and make pretend. I didn't care. I couldn't be real, not with what Joey did to me. But men don't give a fuck anyway. I used to sometimes get a thousand dollars a week. I lived in hotels and went to bars and got drinks. I dressed nice. Some guys always tried to talk to me, but I didn't pay no mind. I just wanted to be by myself.

Apache protected me, but he disrespected me. One time I had money, and I put him in a hotel. Then something told me to come back. When I went back upstairs he had a fucking young fucking little bitch naked with him. I smacked the living shit out of him, and I told her, "Come on. You're coming with me."

The last time I worked on 42nd Street was '86. I was coming out of the show, and I saw my old friend George. He was going there with his brother Cookie. I said "Hey, Moco!"

He said, "What you doing in there?" I said I was working, and he said, "No you're not. Not anymore." He was that sweet. He took me home with him to his house in New Jersey. After that I didn't see Apache no more.

I stayed with George and his parents in New Jersey for a while. I was glad to be out of 42nd Street. I worked for a plastic company, but that was temporary. Then I was a security guard for at least three weeks—until this lady there got on my nerves, and we duked it out. After that, I just stayed at home. It was a good time, but I keep drinking always. I'm an alcoholic, but there's nothing wrong with that.

I found out I was pregnant in '83, but I still had my period. I said, wait a minute, if I'm pregnant, why am I bleeding? I had a pain in my chest, and they took me to the Jersey Medical Center. That's where my daughter was born. Her name was Lucy. *Nancy rolls down her sleeve to show a faded tattoo.*

How did it feel to be a mother?

It hurt. *(laughs)* I hope you guys could feel that one day instead of us. Lucy looked like a monkey. She had hair all over her body. You know how monkeys are? She was premature, seven months. I said, "That's not my daughter. You better give me my kid." Moco, George, was right there with me. He said, Nancy, "That's you're baby," and I said, "No it's not. Give me my baby, goddamnit!" She left me half bald when I was pregnant. I had to wear a hat all the time. But after a while Lucy turned normal and so did I.

George died from water in the brain when Lucy was one year old. After the funeral I gave custody to the grandma. That's all she wrote. I saw Lucy last year. She's a good girl, and she goes to church. Sometimes I want to call her on the phone, but I don't have the number.

After George died, I couldn't stay with his family no more. I got me an apartment in a housing project in Brooklyn. I got SSI. It was all right. I stayed there for three years. I just hang out and get drunk. The hardest thing was that my doggie, Shaquia, bumped the bolt and locked me out of the house. I sat there all night, and the next day the cops had to break the lock to get inside. After that, I didn't have no lock on my door.

Right after that is when I jumped in the East River. I was down in East River Park and it was hot. I seen the water was smooth, but that was a lie. The current smacked me against the wall. My boyfriend Luis jumped in and pulled me out.

When my ID fell in the East River, I couldn't cash a check. After that, I got rid of everything one by one. I sold my radio, my TV. I didn't even care. I had a bar set that I sold to my next-door neighbor for ten dollars. When I couldn't pay my rent, they evicted me.

Nancy is growing tired, and I decide to let her rest. I don't get a chance to record her again for another month. When I approach her on the bench, she is surrounded by a group of young men. One of them had offered to sell me heroin a few weeks before. He eyes me suspiciously as I speak with Nancy. With chest protruding, he casts a cold stare straight into my eyes. "Give me two dollars!"

I thrust my tape recorder into my pocket and say I don't have any money. When I look down at the man's jacket, I see that he also has something sticking up in his pocket— which probably isn't a tape recorder.

"Well you can give me two dollars, or I'm gonna cut your face. That's the only two things that are gonna happen."

Nancy pleads with the man to sit down, but he only repeats his demands. When he notices my concealed hand, he asks, "What you got in your pocket?"

One of my greatest fears is being mistaken for an undercover narcotics officer. For a few seconds, I stand dazed, wondering whether I should run or strike the man with my tape recorder. Instead I pull it out slowly. "I'm a journalist. I'm writing a book about Tompkins Square, and Nancy's going to be in it."

My response seems to catch him off guard. The tension lifts. "You're writing a book? No shit? Can I be in it?"

Yeah. You can be in it.

Nancy is visibly upset with the man and loudly berates him to go away.

That's my nephew. He knows that if I get hype, I'm going off. I don't care if you're my nephew. You leave my friends alone!

It takes Nancy a few moments to relax. A pedestrian stops by with two small dogs, and Nancy holds both of them in her arms while I snap her picture. After she regains her composure, we sit back down on the bench.

After I got kicked out of my apartment, I met my second husband, Curtis. Me and him was buddies on the corner drinking, but he only drank coffee. He was like a big brother. He's way older than me, but there's nothing wrong with that. I moved into his studio in Greenpoint. We had a curtain in the middle. I had my TV and he had his. Most of the time he went out, 'cause he works construction. When I broke my leg, he would jump through the window and help get me in my wheelchair. Then I would sit there till one of the Polacks came and got me. They're very nice people.

After Curtis, I moved in with Pedro. He was a mechanic. Then I moved in with Julio. He drove the cart at the airport that put the bags on the plane. He got me pregnant. After Julio, I met Benny. He was all right, but he had a shotgun. I didn't like that. I slept in the living room. Benny was nice until I was eight months pregnant. He pulled me off the couch, and I hit that little table. I got up, opened the door and kept walking. I went back to New York and moved in with Pedro again. The baby was by Julio, but Pedro didn't care, and Benny don't mind, because all my family's sensitive.

I had twins, Jessica and Jasmine. *Nancy shows another tattoo.* They died in the hospital. That was very hard. I lived with Pedro for nine more years. We had two sons. They lived with their grandparents, but they would visit us on weekends. They were very quiet when they came over. They didn't like it. One day, Pedro shot a lady for money and got two thousand dollars bail. He's upstate now.

Ever since then, I been sleeping around here. I've got good friends out here, and that's good enough for me. I make sure that I have cardboard when I lay down on the streets—if nothing else at least that. People steal my bags sometimes, but nobody hurts me. I can't get no check now, because I don't have ID. The only thing I have is this paper from the hospital. *Nancy removes a prescription for an inhaler. Her address is listed as "Undomiciled. New York, NY 10000."*

Right now I have to panhandle. It might be slow, but it's not very hard. I can get maybe thirty dollars in a day. That's good enough to buy beer and cigarettes. I drink a lot of beer. Give me a case. I'll drink you under the table. *Nancy is rather drunk by this point.*

I live on the streets. There's nothing wrong with that. Indians just sleep in the street. We can't deal with anything else. Fucking immigrants, mother fuckers. I wish everybody go back where they belong and leave our family alone. Just go to damn hell. Right now I'm living on a burial ground from us Indians. Lot of Indians in this ground, and people still take advantage of us. I just wish you all go back to your country and leave us alone. The fire will get you sooner or later. Amen.

I'm sorry. I don't mean that.

In early December Nancy tells me that she's pregnant with twins. In February she tells me that she miscarried. I continue to visit with Nancy. Not much has changed.

Rino Thunder

Sahwachee, Colorado 1935

My mother is the earth. I have four sisters, one for each direction of the wind. My oldest brother is the ultimate warrior, the sun. The trees are my cousins. My grandmother is the moon, and she sees it all. My grandfather, he saw it all begin. No one has ever seen him. You have to give respect. Tompkins Square Park used to be a Manhatty Indian cemetery,* so did Washington Square. There's a lot of confusion here, because the spirits get angry. But the spirits also bless us.

Rino is the undisputed patriarch of the Living Room. All respect his calm, stoic presence, and his history as an actor makes him somewhat of a celebrity with the locals. The first time that I sit down to talk to him, a stranger passes by on a bicycle and announces, "You're talking to a great man!"

Rino is very reserved about discussing his past, and after six sessions I still have a hard time establishing a coherent chronological structure. His voice flows in a slow, deliberate tone, and he tends to repeat his stories. He is particularly fond of talking about the time he won a thousand dollars in a pool game on the Bowery in the late seventies. Each time he tells the story with a different twist.

As one of the park's oldest residents, Rino takes every opportunity to offer guidance to his younger peers. When someone shouts a lewd remark at a passing female, he always reprimands the lack of decorum. Rino becomes absolutely infuriated when people flick cigarettes out into the walkway, and he always proceeds with a drawn-out lecture about a time he saw a dog step on a cigarette and burn his foot. Even I am

---

*Prior to development, Tompkins Square was a swamp.

*not immune to Rino's preaching. Each time that I leave, he
reminds me to call my mother.*

*Rino is plagued by many health problems. He walks with
a cane, and has tremendous difficulty moving about. When
his cane is stolen in late July he simply crawls into the bushes behind the bench and falls asleep. Rino's most embarrassing problem is that his diabetes makes it very difficult for him
to control his bladder. This is particularly true when he is
drinking.*

I was born by the Colorado River in a town called
Sahwachee. My father was from the Ute tribe, the
mountain people, and my mother was a Mexican
American. I was the eleventh child. My parents were
strong and strict, but I loved them. We used to fish
with blankets. Four people would grab the corners
and take it down to the river. Then we would pull the
fish out with respect. There was always plenty to eat.
Now they make you use a hook.

We didn't go to church, because our church was
all around. You felt the energy of the Great Spirit
everywhere. It was about respect. We told many stories. A lot of them got lost in the wind because people
forgot to mention them, but I heard the truth in what
I listened to, and it stayed in me. My favorite story was
about the wolf and the mountain lion:

The mountain lion was the biggest and strongest
animal in the forest. All of the other animals were
afraid of him, but the wolf had wisdom. When the lion
said that he was hungry, the wolf said, "Follow me,
and I will show you the way to the river." The wolf
didn't have to be afraid anymore, because he had a
shadow behind him. When they reached the river.

The wolf asked the lion what kind of fish he wanted to eat. The lion said, "The one I can catch." Then they both had plentiful to eat. You know why? Because they shared. For many years they stayed together and became brothers.

That's what men forget today.

When I was eighteen I joined the Air Force. I ended up being stationed at a base in London, England. I had the qualities to be a leader, but there was too much friction with ignorance. Everybody wanted to be a chief. One night I was out at a bar, and I spoke to a man who wanted to use my picture for a life insurance advertisement.

When I started getting jobs with magazines, I quit the Air Force. I had a good agent, Tim Buckwell and Associates, one of the best in the business. Back then my name was Manuel Escangaleria, but my agent told me that Latinos weren't really in, and I should find a more Indian-sounding name. I got Rino from my middle name, Separino. It also means fire in the Indian language. I got Thunder, because when I was born, my grandfather said I was making thundering noises.

They flew me all over Italy and Spain to do photo shoots. When I got back to the United States they wanted to use me in some cowboy movies. I always played the chief. People like to say that I was a movie star, but it was just a job. Everybody is an actor. It's all just bullshit. But it's a good art. You can control the myth. They hired me for my face, but I think I gave them something more than that. I was very unique.

It was good money, but I didn't always like doing it. You would go into a job, and right away they would start calling you chief. No respect. Don't call me chief.

If anything, I'm a chump for working for you. I'm a man just like you are. I don't call you Mr. President. After a while, I stopped accepting parts where I was being the bad guy Indian. Eventually they labeled me as being difficult to work with. But today I still get five hundred dollars a month from the Screen Actor's Guild. *Rino hesitates to give me any specific details about which movies he appeared in.*

While I was acting, I was involved with the American Indian Movement. There were some good warriors, but the women were the most powerful, because they had wisdom. A lot of the men were full of shit. They were just out for power, like fuck the white boy. They didn't realize that there were a lot of white people on our side.

We are all individuals. The only one you can correct is yourself. No one else can correct you. In 1981 they put me in San Francisco. They wanted me to speak to the children. I asked them, "Do you want me to speak to the children the way that you speak to yourselves?" All that I wanted was a plane ticket back to New York. Columbia University and NYU wanted me to speak, but I had nothing to say, and I would not tell them lies. That just got too much for me, then they said I was difficult. I was banned from them too. They did me a favor. Hell, I was born alone, and I'm going to die alone. I didn't care, because I had crossed the river. That's when I learned I could walk on water. You know how?

When it's frozen.

Rino pauses for a moment to allow his sentiments to reverberate. A police van sneaks up behind us, and the officer catches Rino drinking a beer. "What's going on with that

*beer? You got ID, chief? Come over here." Rino tells the offi-
cer that he can't walk.*

*"Well you had to get in the park somehow, if you can be
in here drinking, then you can walk over and get a ticket."*

*I casually approach the police van and discreetly explain
to the officer about Rino's bladder problem. He responds. "I
know. It stinks over here." The van drives off.*

You see what I say? There's no respect.

I still had money after I quit acting. I had a penthouse apartment on top of a four story building on
10th Street. Back then I had three girlfriends. They
walked away, but to this day in my heart they're my
friends. They were very kind to me. One's name was
Joanne Richards. She said Rino, I love you, but I can't
take this. You're drinking too much. I said that I
understood. Thank you for being my friend. She
ended up getting married to a multimillionaire from
Montana. He had a lot of land and cattle. They came
to visit me one time, and I asked her, "What do you
want Joanne? Add more to the pain?" She said she
only wanted to see the man that she knew before. I
wish her the best. She was a beauty. She made my
heart dance when I looked at her.

After that, I started drinking more and buying
cocaine. Pretty soon I couldn't pay my rent. In 1998
they came in with trucks and put all of my stuff out on
the sidewalk. I fucked up. I can't blame nobody. I
gave my dogs and cats away. They're down in
Connecticut in a good home. I miss them, and I hope
they remember me. I imagine they do.

I'm an alcoholic. I started drinking when I was
twelve years old. There was a man called T. Texas
Tyler. He composed a tune that I really admire

because it was the truth about alcoholism. "Here stands the glass. Fill it up to the brim. Let my troubles go dim." My oldest brother could pluck a guitar like nobody's business. His ego didn't get in his way. He played in Denver and Utah, and he was good. What killed him was the alcohol. But that's destiny. Destiny you can't do anything about. You might say you want to stop, but it's all a myth. I stay in the park because of the devil. He's my favorite uncle. He'll never lie to me.

I call these benches Babylon. These people will be friends with each other one day, and then the next they'll be fighting over nothing. They can't open their mouth without cursing. When a woman walks by, they always say, "Hey, Mamma. Hey, Baby." What if it were your daughter or your granddaughter passing by. There's no truth in that.

I don't talk to a lot of people, because they don't have much to say. Not that I do, but they're full of shit, and they're not good at it. I'd rather listen to the birds sing. I always feel close to the animals. They have respect. They're my best friends and never tell lies. I never sleep around people.

The doctors want to put me in a home. They say that I don't have much longer, but that's not for me to decide. I don't want to be in a hospital. I want to die out here—on the street. That's my destiny.

At the end of my last session with Rino a middle-aged man clutching a bottle of liquor sits down next to us. He introduces himself with his full name.

Rino: Rino Thunder. In Indian Rino means fire. Welcome to my country. *(laughs)* But, you know what? It's not my country. I belong to the country. When I was little we used to go to the Colorado River and fish for rainbow trout. You know how we fished? We got a blanket and put it on the banks and pulled it up. The little ones we used to throw back.

Rino chatters with the stranger for a while about the different types of trout. The man's voice trembles in obvious distress. Rino asks him what's on his mind.

Stranger: On July 13th my girlfriend was murdered. I was the first one to find the body. I have no alibi. Her name was Julie Holden. I loved her so much. We finally decided we were gonna get married, then somebody opened up her neck from ear to ear. When I came into the house, I smelled something horrible. I knew that smell—the smell of death. My heart started beating so hard. I ran upstairs, and I was in such a state of shock that I wanted to kiss her, say good-bye to my baby doggy, my baby doggy, my baby doggy . . .

Rino (with conviction): You're gonna make it, partner.

Stranger: When the police came to take me into custody, I ran. I took a thousand dollars out of the bank and got on a bus to New York. *The stranger reaches into his pocket and pulls out a wad of hundred dollar bills.* I ran up a five hundred dollar bar tab at Sophie's last night. I came to New York, because this is where I grew up. *Tears begin to stream from his eyes.* I'm sorry. I'm sorry.

Rino: No! Don't ever be sorry. Tears are clean. There's nothing to be sorry about when you're crying.

Stranger: Men aren't supposed to cry.

Rino: The hell they're not! Warriors cry. Even when they come from the center of the river where the waves are made of fire, they still cry.

After Rino consoles the stranger, the two engage in a discussion about old-time movies. Rino never lets on that he had been an actor. When I return an hour later, the stranger is being handcuffed and taken into a police car.

In late November Rino falls while trying to get up on the bench, and a pedestrian calls an ambulance. Rino stubbornly refuses to let the paramedics put him on the stretcher. An EMT offers to buy Rino a pack of cigarettes if he complies, but Rino remains glued to the bench. Ten minutes later, a police officer arrives. He is very gentle in dealing with Rino and eventually convinces him to comply on his own accord.

In May of 2002 Rino is released from Cabrini Medical Center and returns to Tompkins Square in a wheelchair. Every night his friends wheel him out of the park onto the sidewalk. Each time I approach, he asks me to buy him a beer. When I refuse, he becomes upset. "Don't play God!" *he pleads.*

The last time that I speak to Rino, he is drenched in rain, sitting in his wheelchair underneath the awning on 7th Street. The air is thick with the pungent stench of urine and feces. I pull out my manuscript and begin to read his story. When I question him to fill in the chronological gaps, he incoherently reverts to the story of the pool game on the Bowery. When he is finished, I gather some cardboard from the dumpster and help him out of his chair. It is the first time he has left its confines in two days. As I bid goodbye, Rino raises his voice in trembling song.

"Here stands the glass. Fill it to the brim. Let my troubles go dim. . . ."

Rino was taken back to the hospital two days later.

Initially I was very skeptical about Rino's credibility as an actor. I typed the name Reno Thunder into Internet search engines with no result. When I tried spelling his name with an I instead of an E, I was connected to a web site featuring prominent Native American actors. Rino has appeared in dozens of movies from the sixties to mid-nineties. You can see him in action with Charlie Sheen in the movie Hot Shots *and Robert Duvall and Matt Damon in* Geronimo: An American Legend. *Visit www.curbside-press.com to see pictures of Rino on screen.*

Gray Wolf

Hila River, Arizona 1947

Gray Wolf is a man of extreme ecstasy and extreme sorrow. One minute he's dancing wildly through the center of the park, and the next, he's sobbing softly in isolation. He seems to completely lack a middle ground. Rain or shine Gray Wolf walks around shirtless, announcing his presence with the scattering trills of his flutes. A tremendous extrovert, he is one of the few regulars who associates with both with the old-timers on the Living Room and the kids on Crusty Lane.

I first encounter Gray Wolf in late June while interviewing Rino. He approaches the bench in a jubilant swagger clutching a forty-ounce bottle of beer. He waits for a pause in the action and then announces in a joyful tone:

This is Rino Thunder, the one and lonely. Du wop, Du wop. I hope he don't grab that cane and hit me in the head. Where did you get this? *(points at Rino's immaculate but outdated polyester suit)* That's the cutest thing I've ever seen on you.

Rino: Someone gave them to me. They'll keep me warm tonight.

Gray Wolf: You're welcome to come home to my teepee. There's two girls—too many for me. Would you like one? No? You got too old for that? It just hangs there and doesn't go anywhere. We'll try to get you some Viagra.

Last Thanksgiving, I listened to your heart, and it sounded like an Indian drum.* Nanna sanna yea,

---

*I later learned that Rino and Gray Wolf were in rehab together at the American Indian Community House. This statement may allude to an experience in therapy.

sanna yea. *Gray Wolf holds his arm up against Rino's.* Hey you're darker than me. You're turning into a brother. *(laughs)* I love you man. *Gray Wolf leaves to go bum a cigarette. Once we're alone, Rino has this to say about him:*

Gray Wolf is full of shit. He talks so much shit he believes it. He's a good man, but sometimes he should just be quiet. It's really annoying when you know that he's intelligent. Maybe someday, Gray Wolf will be able to teach me something, but I'm not sure. There are a lot of other Indians out here, and most of them are full of shit. Sorry to say that, but the truth hurts.

Gray Wolf returns with his cigarette and begins to unburden his conscience:

I can't see my daughter, because I'm afraid that if she sees her daddy, she's not going to be able to let go.

Rino: You blame that on you. You fucked up.

Gray Wolf: It IS my fault. I fucked up royally. I didn't take care of Sara like I was supposed to. The day my daughter was born, I was caught in Arizona.

Reno: Every woman that walked by, you say, "Hey mamma!"

Gray Wolf: I wasn't making love to anyone here. I was just flirting. Like *(turns to lady on next bench)* "HEY GORGEOUS! YOU WANNA GO SOMEWHERE AND DO IT?" *The woman smiles. A tattooed East Village hipster, she is embarrassed, but not offended.*
I was just joking around. I didn't mean any of it.

Sara knew it. She says she wants me to go through a MICA program, Mentally Ill Chemically Addicted. I'm not mentally ill. I'm a professional writer and a musician! How much music do I produce in a year? I've been playing guitar professionally since I was seventeen. That was my first cigarette. My first beer. Not my first woman. I had that when I was eight. *(laughs)*

Throughout these exchanges, my tape recorder is in plain sight, but I'm not sure if Gray Wolf notices. When he sees me recording the next day, he asks about the project.*

Wow! You're writing a book. I had this vision come to me in a dream. Maybe you can put it in there. *Gray Wolf proceeds in the calm punctuated manner of a medicine man, yet maintains the crisp intonation of a New Yorker. Imagine Joe Pesci doing Chief Seattle:*

I was standing on a cliff, and I saw a full moon and a little girl with blond hair sighing in the wind. She's turned backwards so you can see an old dirty white dress. There's an old oak tree at the bottom of the cliff, and you can see the lights of a city far away in the fog. Then there's this wolf call, uuWWWUUUU uuWWWUUUU. She says, "Who am I? I asked the trees, the leaves and the earth. Who am I? I asked the ocean, the waves and the rocks. Who am I? I asked the moon and the stars. Who am I?"

And the wind softly blew into my ear and said to me, "I am very small, but I'm a part of it all." The whole universe—we are a particle—of everything that's created. *Gray Wolf walks away casually, reveling in the afterglow of expanding the consciousness of his fellow*

---

*I later received permission to publish this section.

man. A week later, he bursts into another interview to announce:

The cops don't let me play the flute anywhere in the city! How am I going to make money? The cops arrested me in the West Village for doing ABSOLUTE-LY NOTHING. They took me and put me in the van, and brought me to Broadway. Then they took the cuffs off of me and said go east. "Go east my son!"

Gray Wolf and I speak many times during the next few weeks. I offer to pay him for a longer interview, but he always puts it off to a later date. In late July I bump into him playing his flute on the corner of St. Marks and Avenue A at midnight. Beside him is a graying man with a cane, also shirtless.

Gray Wolf's eyes reflect a troubled mind. He hits me up for two dollars and retreats into the bodega to pick up a beer. When he emerges I follow him down 6th Street. On the way he introduces me to his companion, John Connors. When we reach the parking lot, Gray Wolf sits down and cracks the beer. Before drinking he pours a few drops on the ground and clutches his necklace in meditative reflection.

I was born on an Apache reservation. I was dead when my mother gave birth to me. My whole body was gray. Then, three minutes later, the spirit of a wolf entered me through my nostrils and made me howl uuWWWUUU! That's how I got the name Gray Wolf. My mother was Genera Stormcloud and my father was Jose Ramon Serrano. She was a Navajo, and he was Puerto Rican. They met at NYU. Before they could get married, they moved out to Arizona so that my mother's family could approve of my father. I stayed in Arizona until I was five, and then they brought me here to 13th Street. That's why I got a New York accent.

Years later, I went back to that reservation. I stayed there for three weeks, and they told me that I was chiokawa. I was too urban to be a traditional Indian. That meant I had to go. I was mad, because I wanted to stay and learn more about my people. But I have family here on the streets, and they're one of the best families.

My first family was good too. My parents were great. They were decent to me, and I love them both. My mother used to feed me like you wouldn't believe. If I didn't like what she cooked, she would give me a quarter to go down the street and get French fries. My brother Hector was good to me. He taught me how to talk to girls. When he went into the Army in 1964, he let me keep his dog. We called it Patches after Apache. Do you know what Apache means? Renegade Indians. I speak Apache fluently since I was a little baby.

Even though I lived in the East Village, I went to school up by Dyckman Street way uptown. There were a lot of guidos, *(laughs)* Italian assholes like John. *John laughs.* One of my friends, Whitey, used to bring these little bottles of Seagram's 7 that he got from his mom who was an airline stewardess. Most of the time I was playing hooky to go bowling, but on Wednesday we would go to school just to get sloppy joes. They're the best food I ever ate. I always had girls buy me lunch. After seventh grade I started working.

One day when I was seventeen there was a knock at the door. I saw two Marine officers in green jackets and papers in their hands. They asked to see Genera Stormcloud. One of them took out an American Flag folded in a triangle. When my mother saw that flag, she dropped down on the floor and started crying. I started screaming at the officers, "What did you do to my mother?" Patches bit one of them in the arm, and I had to hold her back. They looked at my mother and said, "Mrs. Genera Stormcloud, we have very bad news for you. Hector was killed in combat. He stepped on a land mine in a rice field." I broke down into tears. As the officers were leaving, they gave me a card and said to call them if I wanted to enlist.

I couldn't accept that Hector was gone. When I turned eighteen, I decided to enlist in the Marines so that I could go over to Vietnam and find him. My mother cried.

I was on the ground for the first two years. It was very high fire with grenades and explosions. I have tinitis in my ears now, it's like someone is kissing your ears. That's why I like sleeping by the train stations. I have a lot of friends who aren't with me now. *Gray Wolf pauses to wipe his eyes and pours another stream of beer on the sidewalk.* They protected my life, and I was ready to die for them.

From '73 to '75, I flew a helicopter ambulance. It was one of the most intensifying helicopters, called the Apache Tomahawk.* It has two machine gunners in the back, radar control behind. My hands had seventeen warhead missiles that could wipe out land from 1st Avenue to Avenue B. Maybe even to Avenue C. Right, John? *Gray Wolf looks to John Connors for confirmation. He silently nods his head.*

On one mission we were flying level, and this guy Sgt. Rock got hit in the head by a bullet from a Mig 28 going mach 3. I yelled, "Tie everybody up, we're

*The Apache helicopter first entered service in 1984.

going vertical!" While he shot two missiles, I shot a
flare. Then I went in through the trees, back up, and
I hit him right in midair. "You son of a bitch!" Sgt.
Rock was my best friend. He taught me how to play
spades on the second level of the *USS Kennedy*.

I got a Bronze Star and two Purple Hearts. I was
shot in my left leg *(pulls up pant leg to show scar)* and my
right hand. The tendons in that hand are made out of
metal. Only four Congressional Medals of Honor
were given to the United States Marines. I got one.
Gray Wolf raises his bottle and toasts John Connors. You
and I made it back here from tensions so deep.

*A teenager with an oversized backwards baseball hat
hovers over the conversation.* "Yo, So you guys are ex
Marines?" *he asks.*

Gray Wolf and John answer in unison. No such thing
as an ex Marine. *Gray Wolf continues.* Once a Marine
you're always a Marine. I'm just retired.

*"So why didn't you stick out?" asks the onlooker. Both
John and Gray Wolf explain that they were injured and
forced out of the Corps. John hands the youngster a VA card
to back up his story. Gray Wolf claims that his wallet was
stolen* and invites the onlooker to sit down. He introduces
himself as Joey. The two exchange an intricately orchestrat-
ed handshake. Joey inquires suspiciously.* "You're Blood?"

I'm a Nieta.

*"Nietas don't shake hands like that, they shake like this.
I know, because I was just smoking weed with one of your*

---

*A reliable source has informed me that at one point Gray Wolf did possess
a VA card.

Niemanitos." Joey presses Gray Wolf's knowledge of street gangs in general. The two disagree feverishly about the representation of various gangs within the deck of cards. Gray Wolf claims that the king of hearts represents the Nietas. Joey claims it for his own gang, Garbodi, because, "Garbodi are about love." Joey adds clout to his position by staking his claim as a Garbodi Elder. Gray Wolf retorts by telling Joey that he is the acting president of the Nietas. "All right," responds Joey, "This is something that all Niemanitos are supposed to understand. Who is the original man?"

I am. Ever since Carlito De Los Hombras died. Bro, I can name every one of the original Nietas: Flaco Vigote...

"No!" Joey's voice picks up in tempo and intensity. "You supposed to know from the scrolls that the original man is the Asiatic Black Man! The maker, the owner, the cream of the planet earth, the father of civilization and god of the universe. All right? You supposed to understand."

Joey continues to test Gray Wolf's knowledge of the Nietas. Gray Wolf counters with rapid bits of Spanish. Joey returns some strained phrases, but Gray Wolf is the clear victor. Eventually the two concede that the details don't matter as long as they stand together on the concept of "One Love."

Joey offers a final tidbit of wisdom into my tape recorder before doggedly pursing an east bound blonde. "Everybody equals one. You've got to unite as a nation. Not even the devil can stop that. That's dead ass."

Gray Wolf returns from urinating on the fence and fixes his eyes mournfully on the crisp summer moon.

There's a sadness so deep, buried inside of me. No one can take it out, not a woman, not even a God can take it out—the pain of losing my mom. That's the most pain I ever felt. *Gray Wolf's eyes begin to well up and his voice begins to shake.* She died on April 15, 1981 of a heart attack. My father didn't want her to be buried, because Apaches are supposed to be buried above ground so that the spirit can go home. The sky was black. My tears shot out like they could hit that tractor-trailer across the street. I laid under a tree by her grave and a patch of sky opened up and poured down bright beams. When they sang the funeral song, I could hear my mother's voice.

After that, I was sad for every day until I met my wife eight years ago at the American Indian Community House at 404 Lafayette. We had Ritchie Havens performing on the second floor in front of a whole society of ancient Indians. I went down to smoke a cigarette, and I saw Sara down there and I brought her in for free.

Sara got me straight and got me to go to programs. I loved everything about her—her body, her smile. Her face is so incredible. She can make so much mischief with her face. I fell in love with her immediately. Every song that I write is for her.

Sara and I don't get along so good now. She still lives around here, and sometimes I go visit her and my daughter. We argue a lot, because she thinks I drink too much.

Gray Wolf is growing tired, and he asks that we continue the interview some other time. I offer him ten dollars, but he refuses to take it. Gray Wolf disappears two days after our interview. Some people tell me that he was arrested, while others say that he went to rehab. One told me that he was dead. I have not seen him since.

John Connors

Australia 1935

John is surrounded by a serene glow as he listens to Gray Wolf ramble on.* When Gray Wolf passes out at two in the morning John is still energetic. He accepts my offer for an interview with coherent enthusiasm, and his words slip through the sweltering air with a content glimmer.

I was born on a military base in Australia. When I was four, we moved to Maryland. My childhood was beautiful. My parents were very caring, and I looked up to them for guidance and support. I got a good education—graduated high school. I could have gone to Georgetown University, but instead I enlisted in the Marine Corps. My father was an ex Marine Colonel, and I wanted to follow in his footsteps.

After ten years in the Corps, they sent us to Vietnam. I went over with a bunch of buddies, but only three of us came back. I did three tours, but I don't like to talk about it much. I saw a lot of action. Thirteen years, seven months, and four days in the United States Marine Corps. I got out a sergeant, E7. I wanted to make a career out of it and get my twenty years in, but I was discharged honorably for medical reasons. I've got two Purple Hearts and a lot of metal in my legs and hands.

Coming back after the war was a nightmare. I lost a lot of friends. People would spit in your face and call you baby killer. Not too long ago some guy in the park was talking all sorts of trash about the Vietnam Vets. I didn't even tell him I was there. I'm not proud of killing people. I also didn't appreciate that fucking

*John would later admit that he was aware of various inconsistencies in Gray Wolf's story.

parade for Desert Storm. You don't have a parade after a war. When my father came back from his war the people all embraced him. It wasn't the same for me.

When I came back from Vietnam, I moved to New York and started working for my dad's firm. After a while, I just couldn't deal with everyone giving me orders. I don't know what it was, but I just couldn't stand being inside. I started sleeping out on the street for weeks at a time. My wife couldn't take it so she ran off with another guy. I don't blame her. She just couldn't deal with me being out on the street.

After about a year of sleeping outside, my family got me to move back into their house in Maryland. I found another wife, and we had two more kids. I tried to make it work, but I just couldn't deal with the stress of being penned down. When I'm inside I feel tied in. I don't like being tied in. I was tied in when I was in the war. I just walked out and went back to New York and lived on the streets.

I love the street life. When you're living on the street, you can do whatever you want. I've been out in the street off and on since 1973. I steer clear of problems. I haven't been in many fights, maybe ten. I've been in war, and I don't want to bring war to where I live. I did a lot of killing. I've killed more people over there than I walked on in New York.

The people I worry about the most are the police. They've been coming down on us harder since Giuliani came in office. I'd really love to see Mark Greene get in there. He's a smart boy. I'd vote for him. I vote every year. Shit yeah. I voted for Koch, David Dinkins. I even voted for Clinton. I loved Clinton. I voted for Hillary, too.

I like the Lower East Side, but it's starting to

change. This used to be a real hippie neighborhood, but now the real hippies can't afford to live here. Now that we got rich people, the police are starting to clean up the neighborhood, and you can't get away with what you used to. I don't blame 'em, if I were paying a thousand dollars a month for rent, I wouldn't want somebody sleeping on my doorstep either.

I just want to live my life where I can do what I want, and nobody's gonna judge me. I've met a lot of good people out here. You've always got to have people who are gonna watch your back. One night about three years ago I was sleeping between 7th and 8th Avenue and somebody hit me over the head with a beer bottle. Since then I try to sleep in a group. It's not hard to find good people. It's just how you carry yourself. You can't just walk in like you own the place. I never claimed to be a leader, and I never want to be a leader. I just want to be a survivor. I can do that out here no problem. There's lots of places to get food. Even in the wintertime it isn't so bad, you've just got to cover up at night. I love the winter. I love the snow.

I guess it's sort of like a family out here. There's a lot of young people out here who I help out, especially the young females. I hate to see them abused, because I've got a daughter. I tell them how to get to a coverage house. Sometimes I send them down to Allen Street to get counseling. I wouldn't want my daughter out here. My son, if he wants to be a little junkyard dog, that's all right with me. *(laughs)*

I don't have to be out here if I don't want to. My military pension is one thousand one hundred and sixty-two dollars a month. After I pay child support, that leaves me with five hundred and ten. When I couldn't pick up my mail, they sent my whole check to my wife. She didn't give me a dime of it. I spoke to her two days ago. We don't get along so good.

I'm still in touch with my family. I write my children letters all the time and tell 'em I love 'em. One of my sons is a police officer in New York and the rest of my brothers and sisters are still down in Maryland. They want me to go south and live down there. I could get out of the streets tonight if I wanted to—right this second. But for now I want to be out here. I don't like it inside. I'm like a paranoid schizophrenic. It's not healthy being inside. You've got to get air.

I've lived a hard life, but I can't say that it was a bad life. I'm going to try and enjoy it for a little bit longer, because I know I ain't got that much more time to go. I've already had three CBA's. The doctors at the VA told me that my heart's real bad and they wanted to put a valve in me. For now I'm just taking this medication. I'm not sure if I wanna go through an operation when I might only have a year or two left.

I don't wanna be a burden on nobody. I wanna die on the streets. When I die, my kids are gonna see ashes. I'll be cremated, 'cause I had too much dirt poured over me already. I didn't really try to hurt anybody, but I did what I had to do for my country. If I passed away tonight, I'd say that I lived a good life.

Before I say goodbye to John, he leaves me an address where he can receive mail. I send him a letter nine months later. He calls me on the phone, and we arrange to meet for a photograph and follow up interview in Washington Square Park. Once John finishes filling in the details of his story, I ask him if he has any plans to visit his family in Maryland.

No. I love my New York. A lot of people take care of me. Besides, I don't like being inside no place.

I'll buy you a bus ticket to Maryland right now.

John's eyes fill with tears as we walk to West 4th Street and take the uptown A train to Port Authority Bus Terminal. Together we wait at the ticket terminal and buy a one-way ticket to Maryland. John thanks me profusely and gives me the phone number for his sister. The bus will not be leaving until well after midnight, so I wish him luck and say goodbye.

Nelson Hall
Philadelphia, Pennsylvania 1946

Freedom
Ain't it splendid?
I would dig it more if I could spend it.
Freedom
Hallelujah lead 'em
My kids would dig it more if I could feed 'em.
Freedom
Thank you Abe
Thank you Martin, Thank you Medgar, Thank
you Malcolm
but I still feel like a slave.
Freedom, education
It don't seem to help my situation.
Freedom, Sunday papers
nothing but the robbers and the rapers.
Freedom, from all the know it alls.

I get more from looking at the chalk walls.
I say I'm trying my best not to hate yah
but you're taking advantage of my good nature.
I get weak, and sometimes I'm not too strong.
But I opened my eyes and I peeped.
I been thinking wrong too long
Brother
Thinking wrong too long
Sister

©Nelson Hall

*Nelson is the undisputed champion panhandler of
Avenue A. I often find him posted outside bodegas shaking a
coffee cup while flashing toothy grins at the rainbow river of
late night revelers. He brashly proclaims his appeals with
uninhibited showmanship.*

TRYING TO GET HIGH
SO I CAN BE A NICE GUY!
LOOKING TO GET STRAIGHT
SO I CAN REALLY RELATE!
LOOKING FOR SOME CASH
SO I CAN REALLY GET SMASHED!
I'M TAKING UP DONATIONS
FOR MY SENSATIONS!
I'M TAKING UP A COLLECTION
FOR MY INJECTION!
CHANGE FOR THE STRANGE!
CHANGE FOR THE INSANE!
CHANGE FOR THE DERANGED!
CHANGE FOR US THAT AIN'T GOT NO
BRAINS!
CAUSE WE LOVE IT—

WHEN THERE'S PLENTY OF IT!

Nelson has various creative routines that he calls "hustles." I once find him clutching a plastic doll shouting:

I NEED SOME CHANGE FOR MY WHITE BABY!
IF YOU DON'T GIVE ME SOME BREAD, I'M GONNA CHOP OFF THIS WHITE BABY'S HEAD!

Despite strained relationships with local shopkeepers, Nelson is known and loved by the park community, both homeless and otherwise, and his easy laughter adds energy to any group he chooses to enter. He speaks his mind freely whether he is straight or sober. The only difference is the degree of clarity.

When Nelson is sober, he possesses the ability to discuss politics and social issues with charming eloquence. I frequently find him talking with people who have apartments in the neighborhood. Some of these neighbors occasionally offer to let him spend the night.

After a few drinks Nelson's ability to communicate drastically diminishes. His eyes assume a vacant stare as he repeats strings of catch phrases followed by intoxicating(ed) laughter:

I'M JUST A NIGGER WITH THE BLUES.
IT AIN'T EASY BEING SLEAZY.
IT'S ROUGH WHEN YOU CAN'T GET ENOUGH.
(ESPECIALLY WHEN YOU'RE TRYING TO GET THAT STUUUUFF.)
HaaaaaaGH!!!

I make my first real connection with Nelson when I bump into him panhandling in front of the Village Farms grocery store in July of 2001. He notices that I have a guitar and asks me to play a tune. I strum out some blues chords while he pours out stouthearted vocals. The sound cuts through the sticky night with raw emotion. Soon dollar bills are flowing into his cup.

As I gradually gain Nelson's trust, he finally consents to an interview. I know that if I talk to him in the park, his vast array of acquaintances will constantly interrupt. Instead I invite him to my apartment on Orchard Street. He sits back easily on the couch as he chain-smokes Marlboro cigarettes.

Although Nelson speaks almost nonstop, it is very challenging to elicit a clear picture of his past. During our ten recorded sessions, there are many times when I suspect that he is not speaking with complete honesty. Looking back, I realize that Nelson was just as forthright with me as he was with himself.

I used to be real homeless. Couldn't even see the light of day. Now, I'm homeless by choice. I still have an apartment in Gravesend, Brooklyn, but I don't feel like being there. Right now I'm going through an emotional upheaval. See, I feel more comfortable out on the street than I am in my apartment. I hang out in the park all day, because intelligent conversation for me is like food. I need it to survive. I can't get that in Brooklyn. People were so narrow minded out there that I wouldn't even tell them that I like hanging out in the East Village. I just said I worked in a warehouse or some shit. Being in Tompkins Square is sort of like running back to the tribe. I can deal with it, but I ain't satisfied.

I was born in Philly in 1946. My mother was a hairdresser and my father ran a cleaning service. We always had money, not a lot, but we could pay the rent.

One day I was watching the Ricky Nelson show, and Ricky asked his father for an allowance. I saw Ricky get the money, so I said, "Pop can I get an allowance?" Next thing you know, Pop gets me in the car. We drive out to some neighborhood I never been before, and it's all white people. He gives me a mop and it's clean up this, clean up that. After we did the shit for a few hours, Pop says, "Here's your allowance son. I just want you to know where the money's coming from."

Pop was a born-again Christian. He was a preacher, but he was a smart man in the sense that he had an open mind. He was always inviting people in other religions to come to the house and talk. Some days I wouldn't go to school, because he'd have a white Christian or a Jew come in, and I'd stay and listen to them. I love my father for that. He was kind, but he didn't hesitate to whip my ass when I got out of line. They would chastise me, but they weren't abusive. See, what I got was called a whipping. If your parents really kicked your ass, they called it a whooping. *(laughs)*

Even though my parents were very nurturing, I never really lived up to their expectations. Nothing they did seemed to affect me. The more they whipped me, the more shit I did. I was an inquisitive child with an artistic temperament. I never fit the mold. I wasn't a programmable person. I had a different way of learning that they didn't understand, and I wouldn't let them beat me down. The only thing in my whole life that ever beat me down was killer pussy.

At school I just sat in the back and drew pictures. I'm dyslexic. I couldn't read until I was twelve. It wasn't that I couldn't teach myself how to read, it's just that I wasn't interested by the materials they gave me. I couldn't take tests. Tests are tricks, very narrow, very checkerboard—A B C D left, right, and look right. A test doesn't give you room to express yourself with it's narrow parameters. True knowledge is an expansive possibility of the human experience. Don't misquote me on that one—I mean that shit.

My teachers were dumb ass narrow-minded racist mother fucking limited people—and some of them were black, sitting up there trying to kick me some shit, trying to indoctrinate me into their scheme. They didn't see my potential. To them I was just a little demon. Fuck the teachers. The only education that I got was out on the streets.

Me and my friends would always skip school and go on a train outside the city. We'd talk to all kinds of people, just like what you're doing now with your tape recorder. Half the time, I didn't even know where the fuck I was at. We'd get stranded some nights and have to walk home. Some nice white lady would say, *(high trill)* "Oh little boys. What are you doing here?"

We'd say, "I don't know. We're trying to get home." Then she'd give us money for the train.

We used to go to Hobo City in Philly on the train tracks. It was mostly old white muthafuckas, drinking their wine, telling us about their war stories and all kind of lies. We knew they were lying, but we didn't give a fuck. Even their lies were true in that we had a true experience listening to them. At least it was better than school. I skipped school as much as I could. I hated it.

My parents were heartbroken when I started

going astray, but they couldn't say nothing. I was an independent person with a creative spirit, kind of like one of these punk kids in the park. I used to have a ring in my nose. I had a little radio, and I walked around playing the pan flute. Bodda dippity do bop, playing jazz and shit. I wasn't trying to freak anybody out. It was just my own expression. I didn't give a shit what nobody thinks back then, and I don't give a shit about it now. Like people in the park ask me, "Why you talking to this white muthafucka?" but I don't give a fuck.*

When I was fifteen I joined a gang. Not a real gang, like the Bloods and Cryps—just a bunch of kids who wanted to get some pussy. We'd get together and practice our cha-cha steps, then we'd go to parties dressed like princes and tear the shit out. Of course we'd walk off with the broads. Now the other boys in the neighborhood didn't appreciate this, so it led to a lot of fights. As I started getting older, muthafuckas started pulling out .45 automatics. I didn't mind punching people in the mouth, but I didn't want to be a part of that, so I said I wanna get the fuck outta here. That's when I started checking out the bigger picture. That's when I met Chuck.

Chuck was this Black Muslim on my street. He was so intelligent in the way that he cut down my little delusions that I was afraid of him. He called me a nassaroni, an ignorant person in Arabic. It took about two years for me to get so I would even talk to him for more than a few minutes. Then one time, he was sitting on the stoop and he said, "Wanna smoke a joint?"

That night was pivotal. After that we talked till the sun rose every night for the whole summer. He told

---

*Once while sitting with Nelson in the park, one of the less pleasant regulars approached him and asked, "Nelson, you got any of those CRACKERS that we were eatin'. You still got that bottle? I wanna drink me a CRACKER."

me things I've never heard of before. It was like being enlightened. He made me read books and newspapers, James Baldwin, JA Rodgers, Benjamin Banaker, Marcus Garvey—all kind a niggers. It was the first time that I really gained an awareness for intelligent men of color, stuff the school wouldn't teach you—stuff that was discredited to make you feel like shit.

Once I started educating myself, I didn't want to hang out with the small-time hustlers on my block no more. I started going down to 52nd Street in Philly. It was a real black area. The hot spot for movie stars and jazz muthafuckas—open twenty-four seven. As a matter of fact, white people were coming in there to check it the fuck out.

That was my introduction to the beatnik scene. I guess what impressed me most about those cats was their reclusiveness. You couldn't just walk into the beat scene and be down. These were some educated people, and you had to feel your way in. I made my connection going to art school on Saturday mornings. It was free. That was something that kept me away from being totally crazy.

When I was nineteen I moved into a loft in Downtown Philly and started exhibiting my paintings at galleries. Everybody embraced what I was doing. I was part of the group that was up on what ever was influential, whatever was controversial—we knew that shit all across the board, black and white. We were some slick-ass niggers.

What's a slick-ass nigger?

A slick ass nigger is a mentally astute individual who refuses to accept the remedial roles prescribed to him by the system.

photo Clayton Patterson circa 1984

I did a lot of hustles, but mostly I'd sell jewelry on the street. One time I was taking some turquoise into a jewelry store, and I started talking to this broad about art. The bitch was killer, both physically and intellectually. She was a sculptress, so her hands just had that healing magic—a white girl, but I think she might have been part black, because her nipples was brown. *(laughs)*

Wendy moved into my loft and we had a nice thing going on. I was getting some extra cash doing paintings on commercial vans. We were living 'n lovin, warm like an oven. *(laughs)* After we'd been living together for a while, Wendy went and told me that she got the rabbit test. The rabbit died.

I was like huh? I didn't know what to do. I knew that I was gonna have to be more responsible, and that scared the shit out of me. The day that my son came out of his mother was the day I became a man. I named him Ashanti after a tribe in West Africa. He was a beautiful kid—deep eyes. I loved playing with him and having him on my back. We used to get paid to pose nude as a family. It was beautiful. We were the quintessential interracial couple.

But that same thing that made us so beautiful was the same thing that started to tear us apart. Wendy's family didn't like what she was doing, and they put pressure on her to stop seeing me. I just came home one day, and she was gone—ran off to California with an old boyfriend. She took both of our children, one in her arms and another inside of her.

I was brokenhearted—crushed. When I found out where she went, I just left all my stuff in Philly and got on a plane. When I got to California, it was me, Wendy, and her boyfriend all living in the same apartment. I tried to be as Jewish as I could about it, a real gentleman, but my heart wouldn't do it. He had been with her, and I knew it wasn't gonna be the same. I tried, but I couldn't have those feelings. She fucked up. I gave her some money, and then I went back to the East Coast. The last time I saw her, I was getting into a taxicab, and she had tears in her eyes.

Were you there to see your second kid being born?

Nelson had maintained a detached intellectual tone throughout the interview. When I ask this question, his voice begins to falter, and he collapses into profuse sobbing.

No. I fucked up. I wasn't at the hospital. I held him once for a little while. He looked more like me than the first one. They named him Michael. I didn't get a chance to name him. I would have named him Attuque. In Swahili it means brilliant and majestic.

It's three o'clock in the morning when we finish our ses-

sion. I let Nelson use my shower, and I give him some old clothes. Before he leaves, I take out my guitar and we make some music. Nelson agrees to sing with me at the Summer Antifolk Festival in Tompkins Square in two days.

On the afternoon of the concert, I find Nelson reclining in his usual place in the Living Room. He is well into a Colt 45, and judging from his slouched posture and slurred words it isn't his first of the day. He is also complaining about having hurt his back while jumping over the fence earlier that morning. Initially he tells me to play the concert without him, but after some prodding, he agrees to take the stage.

A brilliant transformation takes place as Nelson steps up onto the platform. His weary eyes glow with piercing light as he stares out at the hundreds of puzzled spectators. When I bang out the opening chords, he struts toward the microphone with a confident swagger, then erupts:

ONE DAY YOU WAKE UP IN THE PITS!!!
Because your life is full of shit.
And you can't make no sense of it
anymore.
And you think it's so jive
Cause you hardly arrived
And you know you survived,
But you're not certain you're alive for sure.
And you ask yourself
as you pass yourself
in the mirror
Trying to make it clearer.
Is this a human or a rat race?
What makes you think you'd come in first place?
And when you stink an' look a disgrace,
And then you think that you'd be better off if
YOU COULD BE ERASED!!!

And you look around, discover
Every face is like another.
And you find a lover
quicker than a friend.
And you wonder what you're doing
How your life could be so ruined.
How the people you were screwing
Did you end and again.
Ain't it a shame to be lame and out of luck.
Caught in the rain with your pain.
And you ain't got a buck.
Try to explain, they say you're insane,
so they'll lock you up.
Tell 'em your number and name,
but they don't hardly give a fuck.
They don't dare, give a care, about you and me,
YOU CAN'T COME HERE
AND GO TO JAIL FOR FREE!!!

Anyway, you might as well just finish the game.
You're luck's been so bad it can't do nothing but
change.
You might as well play it.
You already got to pay it.
You might as well win it.
Because you're already in it.

(Chorus)
Nothing to it but to do it.
or regret the day you blew it.
Nothing to it but to do it.
You can do it! You can screw it! You can chew it!

And if you really play it,
each and every night and day it,

gets a little better than it was before.
and if you wanna win it,
PUT YOUR SOUL AND BODY IN IT!!!

Take a dare, if you care,
be aware or be square.
You might as well grab it
Or you'll always wish you had it.
You might as well take it,
Cause that's the only way to make it,

(Chorus)

ONE DAY YOU WAKE UP IN THE RITZ!!!
Because your life is full of hits.
You can have your every wish
at the store.
And you think you're so slick
cause you turned every trick
And you did it so quick,
That you can back your tracks
And pick up on some more.

And you dig yourself, as you give yourself
 your desires.
Whatever it requires.
You knew one day you'd make your
breakthrough.
You knew where it was gonna take you.
You knew you'd do what you would have to
You knew one day you'd take the cake
and take the baker with it too.

And you look around and find out,
You would like to take some time out,

so you take another trip around the world.
And you wonder how you did it.
even though you must admit it.
It was a sheer stroke of luck,
that put you up in the bucks.
Anyway you might as well get on with the flow.
You knew what you planted was still gonna grow.
You might as well take it.
There ain't no way you're gonna fake it.
You might as well love it
Cause you're already of it.
You might as well dig it
And live your life the way you live it.

You make the scene and you lean without gravity
Your self esteem's so extreme it's insanity.
Life is a dream and you're living it like a beach.
You're so extreme that your guest tonight is
even Robin Leech.
Bonsoir Robin, entre mon chateau
Life's so much better when you're rolling in
dough.
(Chorus)

And these are the facts,
from the Reverend Doctor Daddy Max.
© Nelson Hall

I don't see Nelson for six weeks after the concert. Word among the regulars is that he has checked into rehab. In late August I find him sitting on the bench with clean clothes and a pair of reading glasses. The rumor was true. Nelson was in an inpatient rehabilitation center and had been clean for more than a month. The facility released him for the weekend before he would check into a follow-up program. Nelson reaches into his bag and pulls out a sheet of paper. It's a letter he had written in rehab.

My dearest and damning addiction,

It's been about a month now since I left you. I know, I should have said good-bye, but it was difficult to do. I hate extended breakups. They don't work. I'm not too good at that. But we were good together for a long time, weren't we? I remember chasing you when you were hard to get. You were so elusive and defied status quo. You excited what was a rebel in my heart. I watched you from afar when others had their joy with you. You were in fashion. You were chic and esoteric. Your elegance, your allure, persuaded me to know you, and when I did, I knew you'd be the hardest to forget. I was completely fascinated, dedicated and committed.

I thought that you were good for me, and for a while you were. You have a way of making me forget about the rougher part of life. There is an instant soothing comfort in your company. But then again your other side offends me to no end. You're just a player with a zero-sum agenda. You gamble for the glory and the guts of your opponent, but you never put up any of your stakes. You're a fraud and an enemy to anyone who takes to you.

You suck. You sucked my precious time and opportunities. You sucked my inclination for achievement and success. You sucked my mind until I was oblivious to everything, causing me to lose myself in reoccurring blackouts. You sucked my dwindling bank account to multiplying debt. You sucked my sense of self-respect and pride and left me begging in the street. You sucked the joy out of my laughter and the lovers from my arms. You tried to suck my health, my very zest for living. At last you have tried to suck my soul, you sucking succubous.

I don't blame you. Sucking is your nature. I was disillusioned and confused. But now I see you clearly for the sucker that you are. I must end our sucking sick relationship at last, and leave you in the shadows of my darker yesterdays and dismal nights. It's time for me to muster all initiatives for life, and rectify the damage that you've done to me for years.

If we should encounter, please make no attempts to reconcile. I simply will ignore you and succeed. So long, farewell, and go to hell. Suck your way to some-one else's sorrows somewhere else. It makes no sense to let you suck me senseless anymore.

Sincerely,
From the one you sucked,
who sacked you for sublimity and courage,

Nelson Hall

Nelson receives many words of encouragement from both the regulars and several well-dressed acquaintances that are passing through. We get lunch at Alice's Restaurant to cele-brate. Nelson is bursting with energy, and he talks my ear off with plans of writing a novel.

When I ask Nelson about his apartment, his easy smile begins to fade. He has not paid the rent in over four months. Tonight he plans on getting on the train and seeing if his key still works.

Two days later I take an evening stroll through the park. Nelson is sitting on the bench drinking a beer.

It didn't work. The key didn't work.

Nelson doesn't have much to say about his relapse, and he tells me to go away. When I question him the next day, he goes on an extended rant about how the counselors at the rehabilitation center were jealous of his creative spirit. He also blames the facility for releasing him on a weekend.

It doesn't take long for Nelson to return to his all-day everyday drinking habits. As summer comes to a close, Nelson is beginning to show signs of mental and physical deterioration.

After I left California, I moved into a squat on Fulton and Clinton down in Brooklyn. It was kind of rough, because we didn't have no heat, but it was good to be surrounded by other artists. I hung out with Fred Floyd, John Mitchell, and a bunch of other hip cats. It wasn't too bad, because we didn't pay rent.

After a year in the squat, I met a waitress in Manhattan. She was gorgeous. I was like, hey baby, we gotta get shit together. That night she put her number on the back of the check. See, I had a reputation for being a lady's man, but really, I was looking for love. My heart was hungry, and I needed somebody to match my sensuality. It wasn't that I was trying to be a player. I just dug killer bitches.

Sophia was from Denmark. She was damn near as tall as me. She was so gorgeous that she looked like she was completely made up, but she never wore makeup. After we went out a few times, I moved in with her on Ridge Street. She was a painter. At first she thought that I was just a poet, but when she found out that I painted too, she was disturbed. She had a lot of soul, a lot of funk, but I was more developed than she was.

We had a tempestuous relationship, real rough

sex, great shit. When I was walking around in art galleries, people always used to ask me why I had black eycs. I said excuse me, but it's part of my sex life. *(laughs)* Me and Sophia's physical shit never wore off, but what made it really bad was the artistic animosity. We were two artists taking up each other's space and dampening each other's inspiration.

One night Sophia didn't come home, and I was alone in the apartment going crazy. I had no idea where she went. Two weeks later she came in. She had a moving company outside, and she told me to move my shit out. I wasn't going out like a chump, but later that night I left on my own terms.

That was the middle of the wintertime and I was on the street. It was harsh. The zipper broke on my pants and my fucking balls were freezing. I got something called a hydrocelic. Muthafuckas swelled up like cantaloupes. Oh man the cold! The holes in the bottom of your shoes open up, and you're walking around in the fucking ice, and there's nothing between you and the cold except your wishing you wasn't on the street. You jump on a train out of town, you try to move around—do something. You go to bars and pull bitches you otherwise wouldn't even talk to. And even if they do look good, they don't remind you of your old lady, because they ain't that fine, they ain't that personal. You get warm but then you're gone, and you're still fucked up, emotionally and spiritually devastated. You're just walking the fuck around. Freezin your ass off. Ain't got no fucking money, cause the day the bitch kicked you out you paid all the fucking bills. . . .

A roving panhandler interrupts our interview. Nelson and I tell him we're broke.

"What the fuck, man?" responds the panhandler.

Hey listen man, if we had money we'd give you a whole bunch. We'd give you a hundred bucks if we had it.

"You—a—muthafucka!" The solicitor's voice trembles in desperate incoherency. Nelson immediately rises to his feet.

Oh yeah? Well you a muthafucka's, muthafucka's cunt! Yeah! Yeah! Yah muthafucka's, muthafucka's cunt!

"Yeah I am! I'm the muthafucka that be busting yo' ass…"

Yeah! You pussy ass, clot blood, clot muthafucka! Now what else do yah want? You want some else shit for a muthafucka? You like some shit?

The man utters a furious reply that is too jumbled to decipher.

Yeah man! You fuck with me, I fuck you up. Yeah, you better get the fuck away from me. Get yo' honey, yo' money, your momma and papa too. You want some shit? Fuck with me! Ha ha! Cause we love it when there's plenty of it! Ha Ha! FUCK WITH ME!!! I'll set you FREE from your MISERY!!!

The man slowly walks away, yelling incoherently. I plead with Nelson to focus on the interview.

Anyway, as I was born and raised in the USA, as I

began to say.

In the springtime one of my boys from Philly came to get me off the streets. He had his guitar and we did a little jam session in Washington Square Park. Damn we were bad. We busted open a squat at 171 Avenue B, and we moved in. It was actually a homestead, because there was one original tenant in the building. We put together a punk band called Vampire State. We played some bars, and we were doing all right, but then Lou Reed stole our drummer. My boy was kind of frustrated, so he split town for a while. I stayed.

Back then Avenue B used to be called the Supermarket. You had people slinging drugs all the way from 14th Street down to Houston. It was open twenty-four seven. On an average night, you'd find hundreds of people waiting in line in front of one door—and you could find hundreds of that. You'd see young girls sitting on top of cars with their legs wide open—putting their pussy right in your face while they're sticking needles in their arms. "You want some pussy muthafucka or you want some drugs?" I'd never seen nothing like that in my life, it was so, so *(pauses)* unique. People used to come visit me from out of town, and I'd take them down to see it. That was the real New York City—way beyond the Statue of Liberty and the World Trade Center.

One morning, I was sittin' in the kitchen drinking my beer, and the ho from next-door came knocking on my door asking if she could use my bathroom to shoot up. She didn't want her pimp to see that she had money. Next thing you know, they were coming over every day. Each time they'd do it, they'd drop me like twenty dollars. Every morning I had a hundred and fifty dollars on the table just for letting the broads use

my bathroom. Bitches was walking all over my apartment half dressed and shit. I'm saying damn, this is all
right, *(laughs)* and I wasn't even fucking these broads.

Next thing you know, I had a house full of bitches and plenty of coke. I wasn't trying to be no mack. It
just came to me, because I wasn't trying to rip nobody
off. Everywhere they went, these girls got ripped off
and beat up. I was treating 'em nice. Anyway, I had all
this shit, and the muthafucka across the hall didn't
appreciate that too much. He was a pussy ass, so
instead of dealing with me like a man, he called the
police. They had ten officers come in and go through
everything in my apartment. The only thing they
found was a spoon with heroin residue, but that was
enough. I had some previous warrants, so they put
me in Northern Facility on Riker's Island for a few
weeks. When I got back out, I was on the street.

Being out on the streets was totally different since
crack hit the scene. See, I was never a real compulsive
crackhead, I just did the shit when it was around. It's
like a neurotic sensation. It takes you all the way up to
the sky like an airplane, and then it throws you out
with no parachute. When you hit the ground you can't
deal with it. Somehow, you just got to get somewhere
between where you was and where you're at. You
don't care if you don't get as high as you was, just as
long as you're not at rock bottom—but I was never a
real crackhead. I never robbed nobody or ate out of
no garbage cans. I just didn't want to be alone, and
smoking crack did something to kill the emptiness.

Three years went by like that, and I started getting tired of it. I started doing a little street hustle*
here and there, and I got me a room on the Bowery.

---

*When I asked Nelson to describe his street hustle, he made me turn my tape
recorder off. The only thing he allowed me to print was that it was a "slight-
ly deceptive appeal to the charitable intentions of the general public."

Gradually I started going to outpatient therapy at St. Marks Clinic. It was no bolt of lighting. I relapsed a bunch of times, but finally I got it. I applied to the Department of Housing, and every day I would give the guy at the desk a couple bucks in case I had any phone calls. One day Housing called and said there was an apartment for me in a project down in Gravesend Brooklyn. 1992 was the most pivotal year in my life. I got a second chance.

My rent was only a hundred dollars a month, so it wasn't that hard to get it together. I was making some pretty good cash selling Street News. In those days you paid like fifteen dollars for a hundred papers, and then you'd sell them for a dollar. Sometimes I made a hundred dollars in a day. Eventually I started writing for the muthafuckas, doing interviews and shit. Me and Lee Stringer used to talk all the time.

After a few years Street News helped me get a scholarship to study art therapy at the New School. The professors kind of dug my perspective, because they was all talking old school, but I came in with some fresh perspective. They were talking about books, but I was bringing in ideas from the street.

Once I got my BA, I started teaching kids at community programs like the Clemente Center on Avenue B. After a few months of volunteer work, I got a paying position in midtown teaching creative writing to homeless kids at a drop-in center. New School taught me a little bit of jive-ass shit, but this job was when I really started learning what it was all about.

These kids came from everywhere, just landed on 42nd Street in a bus—throwaway kids. They would bullshit each other all day about their conquests and street stories, but when you got them to put it down in concrete form that cut out all the jive ass bullshit and made them get down with the truth. It was one of the most rewarding experiences in my life. I worked there until they cut the funding. One minute I was making good money, they next minute they fired me.

Once I lost that job I went back to doing my street hustle. I ended up spending most of my time down in Gravesend. I didn't like it at all. It's an intellectually sterile environment. The only people I talked to were the old men who were just out drinking beer and talking about nothing.

I had gotten my life together, but I was all by myself. I had met a few broads, but being sober, it was like I didn't have the same charisma. I noticed that if I didn't get high, I was an outsider. That beer was always in the back of my mind. In '99 I met this French broad—beautiful blond hair, blue eyes. She was twenty-six years old, and she was a doctor. You can't get no badder than that. Stick on the floor—sports car—badass bitch calling you on a cell phone—jazz playing on the fucking radio. She had killer money, flying all over the world. One night she invited me over to her house for a few drinks. Now this bitch was so fine and so classy that I couldn't throw it out. I blew a lot of bitches before that, and I was tired of it. I figured, I'm with a fine bitch, why not get down.

The next day I was walking down the street with a beer in my hand. It's just natural for me. It really wasn't about her, we weren't like a couple. It was about me. Seven years was a long time to be alone. I guess you could say I fell from grace.

As the weather grows colder I begin conducting my interviews inside the cafés on Avenue A. It is difficult for Nelson and I to find a place to converse, because he has been "86'd" from just about every establishment in the neighborhood. In December I attempt to have Nelson sing with me at bar on Avenue A, and he is thrown out by the owner in a storm of curses. Later he tells me that he fell asleep in their restroom a week before.

In late January Nelson disappears from the park. Some of the regulars tell me that he had gotten into a physical confrontation with the police and was arrested. I contact the Department of Corrections, but they say that there's no prisoner named Nelson Hall. Two weeks later I find Nelson sitting on a staircase in the West Village, clutching a bottle of vodka. He is barely coherent, but manages to explain that he had run away from the cops, and they were looking for him.

Nelson returns to the park two weeks later. His condition deteriorates further when he begins combining hard drugs with his drinking. Each time is something different. One night I find him surrounded by glassy eyed teenagers tripping on ecstasy. A week later he tells me a story about intense psychosis from psychedelics. In February Nelson overdoses on heroin and has to have his heart shot with adrenaline in the ambulance. Nelson tells me that he is careful not to take any of these drugs on a regular basis, but their combined effect greatly diminish his ability to communicate. I have hours of tape during this period that are absolutely useless.

In '99 I just started sitting out on the benches in my project drinking every day. I knew I was only fooling myself, but at least I wasn't isolated anymore. About this time last year, I met this broad Clarice. She was a prostitute who lived in the same building. Now I ain't never been interested in paying for no damn sex, but she was a fine looking broad, so I used to say hello. The more I started talking to her, the more I started to feel her. One day her man was beating her up real bad, so she ran to me and told me her story.

When she was a kid down south, her mom was blown out on coke, and she was pimping her out. When she was twelve years old, she got raped by the KKK, the muthafucking Klu Klux Klan. CAN YOU IMAGINE WHAT IT'S LIKE TO BE A LITTLE GIRL BEING RAPED BY THE KKK?!! I heard that story, and I just felt her. I didn't want her turning tricks no more, so I took her in.

I never felt for somebody like the way I felt for Clarice. Now I've had hookers and all kinds a badass bitches. I used to have one bitch who gave me six hundred dollars in one night. I've had bitches kill muthafuckas for me. But this bitch didn't come to me as a ho. She came to me as somebody who was abused. I did everything I could for her. I stopped playing the game. I was—breathing—for her. It was like what she needed and what I had to give her were the same thing.

What was she looking for?

My heart, my soul—even my rock and roll. Bitch wanted everything. And I gave it to her, anyway she want it—from the front, from behind—from the mind. But she wasn't an intellectual. What we had was spiritual. I rode that ass, day and night, *(laughs)* but for the first time in my life I had something deeper than just a physical connection. Every time we were together it's like we had an electricity. We used to go to bars where everybody was just sitting down and start dancing. We'd get everybody else dancing, and then we'd leave. The shit was slick. What we had was pure joy.

Look at me, man. Look at me. I'm an old ugly muthafucka. I think the only thing I got going for me is maybe some testosterone. If I was a bitch, I would-n't even look at me, but here I was with the finest bitch in the neighborhood. I don't know why she ended up with me. I try to treat people good, so sometimes the karma comes around, but damn she must have been crazy. She was badder than anything you ever seen. *Nelson diverts his eyes to the avenue and points out several "bitches" that Clarice surpasses in beauty.* My bitch was so bad that her eyes changed color according to her mood.

Now, when you're living in a confined black project, all the little dark-skinned bitches think they ugly. I thought they all was fine, but they was conditioned to think that they was ugly. Now my girl, she was light skinned, and she knew she looked good and didn't mind showing it. She was always trying to out hoochi-fy all the other bitches—always had her skirt just a lit-tle bit shorter or her shirt just a little bit tighter. She was so fine, all the broads wanted to beat her up—Brooklyn style. They wanted to cut her face off. Now, my girl was street wise, but she wasn't street mean. She had a good sense of herself, but she didn't know how to deal with that type of situation. She had this one fight with another bitch whose man was in the xxxxx gang. I had to step in and stand up for her, and that made the shit get really heavy.

One night a bunch of xxxxxs came and kicked the shit out of the both of us. I was fighting ten cats, they had a fucking gun upside my head. The next day we got on the train and went to go stay with some of my people in Harlem. I went on a three-day alcoholic binge, and we got split up. I ended up coming down to Tompkins Square, and I ain't seen her since. People said she came looking for me, but we kept missing each other. Since that shit went down, I haven't been able to get it back together. It's like I'm a man in the snow with one shoe on and one shoe off.

That's how I came out here. That's why I got the blues. How did it happen? Cause I gave it all away. My whole life, I never gave it up like that. I might have loved people before, but that was because I needed them. But I was loving her, because I wanted to give her something. It's the same activity but the intention is different. Damn. If somebody fucks over that, you're hurt.

I know that I can go to rehab and put up with all the mind-control shit, and eventually they might put me back in housing. But that's just going to be the same shit. That shit is like living in a tomb, it's like a leech that sucks out your intellect. It's sick—a twisted mentality in an uncontrolled reality.

This ain't no fucking joke. Whatever I gave you, I could write about myself twenty times deeper. I can write the nuances. I can write the tastes and the smells. My story could be disguised as something else. I know how to do that shit. When I first started talking to you I was very protective. I was very careful about hiding my shit. But this is it. This is the real deal. I'm giving it to you, because I'm not sure what's going to happen to me tomorrow.

Two weeks later I bump into Nelson at the chess tables. The minute that I look at him, I see a change. Instead of a blank drunken stare, his eyes sparkle with a glimmer of intelligence. He tells me that he had just gotten out of a seven-day detox at Harlem Hospital. We sit down for dinner and coffee at Alice's Restaurant.

I pull out my laptop and read Nelson his interview. He is embarrassed about some of the things he had said while drunk, but he insists that I leave them in there. When we fin-

ish, Nelson expresses a desire to write an epilogue for the book. The next day I bring him my old laptop, and he invites me to a friend's house on Avenue D where he can live for a few weeks while he writes.

The next time that I see Nelson, he's leaning against a car on Avenue A, extremely intoxicated. I can see in his eyes that he recognizes me, but he's unable to converse. As I reach out to shake his hand, he keels over and slams face first into a mud puddle. A gash over his eye drips blood on the curb. Nelson's friend Juan Ferguson helps me pull his body up onto the sidewalk. We attempt to stand him up, but each time his dead weight collapses. Juan stops some people on the street with a cell phone, and an ambulance comes roaring down Avenue A within minutes.

The paramedics say hello to Nelson calling him by name. They make several attempts to load him onto the stretcher, but he's too heavy. On their final attempt, his pants fall down and the ambulance driver has to pull them up. Some rookie police officers on the scene laugh heartily. Finally, Juan steps in and muscles Nelson onto the stretcher.

My heart sinks as I watch the ambulance pull away. Little do I know that Nelson's story is far from finished.

The Lighter Side of the Living Room

Between my interviews in the Living Room I share many laughs with the regulars. Their tall tales and witty cracks are clearly a coping mechanism to gloss over a greater abyss, but I admit that they provide all of us a much-needed release.

Homeless Shelter Honeymoon

by Radio Rob

I saw two guys getting married when I was living in the shelter down in Washington. They cleared all the beds out of the place and this tall guy who called himself a preacher did the whole damn ceremony. These dudes went all out for the shit. One dude had on a gown. The other dude had a tuxedo. They said, I do, I do, and they exchanged rings. They had a wedding cake and everything.

Some people were like, "How you gonna marry

these goddamn fagots? Shit you know this homeless guy ain't no real preacher." You had a lot of that, but I didn't care, because they had brought in a lotta liquor. I hadn't had a drink all day, so I was feeling all right.

Pretty soon everybody goes to sleep. Now before you go to sleep in a shelter you pick up your bed and you put one post in one shoe and one post in the other shoe. Being that a lot of people were drunk they forgot to do that. Now I don't know how these guys did it, but when we woke up these two dudes were gone, and so was everybody's shoes. I guess they needed finances for the honeymoon, but what the hell are you gonna do with a hundred pair of shoes? Can you imagine a hundred dudes walking down the street with no shoes on? Everybody's feets is stinking to high heaven. Think about how beautiful that would be.

King of the Supermarket

by Juan Ferguson (Ferdinand)
(I don't look like a Juan, do I?)

When I used to return my cans at the Associated
Supermarket, sometimes the manager would give me
a few bucks to help sort out the big bags in the basement. One night I was down there sorting the cans,
and I fell asleep. I heard them pulling the gate down,
and I ran up there but it was too late. I tried to open
the door, but it was locked from the inside too.

At first I was mad, because I don't like to be
locked up inside no place, but then I started looking
around and saw all the different kinds of food. I
walked through the isles and there was nobody anywhere. I said, "Shit, this ain't too bad. I'm gonna take
advantage of this beautiful world."

First thing I went to the deli and took a big bite
outta the roast beef. Then I got a bucket 'a potato

salad. After that I went over to the pickles. I come around to the beer section, and they've got twenty-five different kind a beers. I must have drunk nine or ten beers, then I put all the cans in my bag so I could take 'em back the next day. Then I went up to the back room and fell asleep.

I slept for a few hours, and then I went back down and started all over again. I had a big duffle bag and I went and got some more food and beer. I must not have realized what time it was, because when I went back to the room the manager was coming in. He looked real surprised to see me.

"What are you doing in here?"

I started laughing, and then I said, "I got something on you." And you could see the fear in his eyes. "Oh Yes. You locked me in here last night." And right at that moment, you could see his face change. Now, I was the manager, and he was the employee. He didn't wanna get in trouble for what he did, so he just let me walk right out the door.

I came back that day to return the cans, and nobody said nothing, because for that night, I was the King of the Supermarket.

The Solution

Alvin T. Walker Jr.

Alvin T Walker Jr.
The Escape Artist

alvin@curbsidepress.com

I've been out on the street since April. I was working at a warehouse, but I got laid off, and I couldn't pay my rent. You go to a lot of these programs, and the first thing they want to do is stick you in a rehab program or make you see a psychologist. But I don't do drugs, and I'm not crazy. I'm out here because of the simple fact that I don't have a job.

Right now I'm trying to focus on my artwork. I've been working on a series of comics called The Comic Script Story Board, and I'm hoping that somebody's going to pick them up. I got a positive attitude, and I'm not afraid of being out on the street right now, because God is with me. Though I be streeted, I'm not defeated.

Just

I'm good-spirited. Trying to make it. Life is not easy. It was never easy before this, and it's not easy now. I got a lot of issues with addiction, but I also got a lotta distaste for the American System—a lot of anger.

Milton Irby
Don of Tompkins Square

I'm a courteous person, and I've got a heart. I don't care what color you are. If you treat me real, I'm gonna treat you real. You treat me fucked up you gonna get the same shit coming back at ya.

These are my best friends. I don't care how far up the ladder I climb, I'm not gonna never forget these guys. If I could get me a house, my door would always be open. These are my friends, and I don't give a fuck about what else. *Milton was one of several regulars who received a fifty-dollar bill from Muhammad Ali on Christmas 2002.*

Uncle Vinny Harcuail

Vinny has lived around the park for twenty years. Last winter he had a tumor removed from his tounge. Although his speech is somewhat impeded, his thinking is coherent.

I ran away from an IRS *(Indian Reservation School)* in Nova Scotia when I was sixteen years old. I was talking Micmac, and the nuns beat the hell out of me. I got tired of fighting with the Frenchman, and I said let me get the hell out of here. I been living here ever since.

Robert Romero

I woke up this morning, and I was dead broke. I turned around on the bench, and guess what I found—a hundred dollars. When you're not a bad person God always helps you somehow. So, today me an Vinny been drinking Thunderbird. Nothing wrong with that. When you go to church and you get communion, they give you wine. When I was an altar boy, we used to go downstairs and get drunk in the basement.

But the good old days are over. The Lower East Side used to be the Lower East Side. Now it's a rich neighborhood. It hurts me real bad. It's just the rats of the rats that are left.

Mustaffa

I'm sensitive, charitable, sometimes honest—a noble brother I came to the park three years ago. It's a good time. Even if I'm broke I can come here and have me a drink any time. Right now I'm working to get some money to go down to Augusta, Georgia to visit my daughter. I'm not gonna be out here forever.

Mustaffa has since left the park to enter rehab.

Sugar Bear

When I was coming up, I got arrested for sticking up number runners. The police came into my high school and arrested me. I did eight and a half years in jail, and that's where I learned how to box. That taught me some discipline, so I'm not violent outside the ring. I just try to get by, and as long as you show me respect, I'm going to respect you.

photo Clayton Patterson

Stack (right) with friend circa 1989. RIP 2002

Victor and Hot Dog

Crusty Punk Lane[*]

"There's two kinds of punks: house punks, punks that live in a house, and crusty punks, or gutter punks, who live on the street. I guess I'm a crusty punk." —Skunk

If Tompkins Square Park were a school, Crusty Lane would be the smoking stall in the boy's bathroom. This secluded corridor of benches is the central headquarters for a fluctuating corps of younger park regulars. Many openly identify themselves as "punk rockers," while others claim that no label can adequately reflect their unique brand of Dionysian insurgence. Members of this loose knit tribe hail from a vast array of backgrounds. Disgruntled sons and daughters of corporate climbers share these benches with the progeny of prostitutes. Some are illiterate, while others are poets. A few keep records of their travels with disposable cameras and notebooks. Although many people on these benches are addicted to heroin, it is important for me to point out that the majority are not.

Most regulars on Crusty Lane are easily identified by their colorfully dissonant appearance.

"I don't do this because I want people to look at me, I just want to be myself." —Chaos

Some are content to assert their individuality with

---

[*]According to a regular named "Hatred," the name Crusty Lane originated with the officers of the 9th Precinct. Their name for the Living Room is Death Row.

a leather jacket and metal chain, while others go as far as tattooing their faces. Regardless of the how far an individual pushes the envelope, most subjects are reluctant to attach any sort of meaning to their adornments and altercations. This is an uncomfortable topic of conversation and is best avoided.

At first I am intimidated by the regulars on Crusty Lane. I only venture into the area when the park is about to close and the crowd has dispersed. With the arrival of autumn, I notice that many familiar faces begin to disappear. By late October I feel a sense of urgency to interact with the group before they relocate to warmer climates for the winter.

On my first daylight visit to Crusty Lane I make the mistake of wearing professional attire from my day job. One of the regulars comments that I look out of place, then he asks, "You got a badge?" Later that same day, a dealer asks me if I'm looking to score. I tell him that I'm cool. He responds, "Oh yeah, who says you're cool?" I pause for a moment, smile, and then point my index fingers toward the sky.

"You're a cool muthafucka," he replies.

On subsequent visits to Crusty Lane I wear a dirty T-shirt and ripped jeans. Sometimes I walk around with a sandal on one foot and a hiking boot on the other. When it becomes common knowledge that I'm paying for interviews and not arresting people, I soon become very popular within the group. Some subjects take me under their wing and help explain the hidden relevance of the group's interactions.

The most fascinating ritual on Crusty Lane is a tradition known as "elfing." If one of the regulars passes out on the bench, his peers have the privilege of covering his face with profane images etched in permanent marker. In order to avoid getting "elfed," one must remove his shoes before drifting into the arms of Morpheus.

As I become more familiar with the group, I am often invited to follow the regulars down to East River Park after Tompkins Square has closed. The serenity of this environment greatly adds to my subjects' ability to communicate, and the lack of police patrols facilitates boisterous outspurts. Many of the old timers who occasionally venture down to the river liken it to Tompkins Square in the late eighties.

As this book goes to press, I have seen some of the regulars return to Crusty Lane with stories of their winter journeys through the south. There are more new faces than old, and although I maintain email contact with all but one of these subjects, I have spoken to only two of them personally since November of 2001.

Anna
San Francisco, California 1984

Anna is a drifting soul. Travel is her sustenance and salvation. The first words out of her mouth are:

I'm a train hopper.

I first find Anna late one Saturday night as she's sitting on the bench with her dog Rosey and her friends Charlene and Theo. A horseshoe shaped ring protrudes from her nose and her arms are lined with pea green star tattoos. An ancient, dilapidated pair of roller skates is bound to her feet with metal wire. The park is about to close, so we decide to head over to Trinity Church. Anna propels herself forward with tense, erratic strides. Suddenly, she skids to a halt to bend over and pick up several cigarette butts on the sidewalk.

If the pigeons eat these, it'll clog up their asshole, and they'll die.

photo Monte

I found these roller skates in a dumpster. I've been using them all day, but I've also been getting drunk all day. I hope I don't lose my teeth. I almost skated in front of a van. God, I love roller-skating. I just need those teeth protectors, like for boxers.

I grew up in San Francisco. Actually it was a suburb called Bloomfield. It's one of those towns where there's not a lot going on, so people have to invent things to bitch about. Boring. My mom and dad got divorced when I was two. She always had a variety of husbands. There's been four other than my dad. It was really intense, because all the sudden they would come into my life and try to be my dad and tell me what to do.

My mom is a total yuppie accountant. She grew up really poor, and she always wanted to do better, but she took it too far. She was obsessed with making money and trying to get me the things that she didn't have. I ended up getting money instead of affection. She was never around. Like I learned how to cook at the same time I was learning to read.

There was a lot of trauma in my early years. When I was five, my cousin used to baby-sit me. He'd to tell me that my teddy bears would hate me if I didn't let him have his way with me.

What kinds of things did he used to do?

He used to fuck me. It went on for three years. When my mom found out, she sent me to therapy. It didn't help much. They tried to make me rationalize it, but you can't rationalize something like that. In the end I ended up thinking that there were two people, my cousin, and the guy who raped me. The guy who raped me was psycho, but they're not the same people.

I never really seemed to fit in at home, and school wasn't any different. In elementary school I had glasses, braces, crutches, and a bad perm all at the same time. Everybody called me the Space Monkey, because I was this little turbo nerd. My only boyfriends were special ed—full on special ed— retarded as shit. I'd play with the second graders when I was in fourth grade. I've always been an outcast. That's what I am.

Up until fifth grade I did really well in school. They were going to put me in an honors class, but I turned it down, because I was worried about the way people would look at me. I had enough of being a nerd. By seventh grade, I learned how to be cool, which at the time meant looking cool. You know those tight body suits? I had a good body at the time, and guys used to drop their pencils to watch me pick them up. I've gained weight from drinking beer, but I used be hot as hell.

Middle school was the first time in my life that I was ever really happy. I met this girl named Cindy who was popular and actually liked me. We got along good because we hated everything and just wanted to say fuck it to everything. We did things our way. Like we'd go to school in pink tutus with sequins and a big bow. They called us the retarded lesbians, because we were always together. We weren't really lesbians. When I was twelve, I slept with my first guy.

My mom was really upset when I first started getting in trouble. She would yell at me, but I didn't care. She just had to deal with the fact that she didn't understand me, and it was too late for her to connect. Eventually she just sort of accepted that I was always going to be out there and original, and she had no control.

Anna's friends show up and drop off a beer. She tells them that the interview is too personal for them to listen, and she'll meet them in East River Park. I promise to walk her there. Charlene casts me a wary eye and suspiciously walks away.

When I was sixteen, I just decided I had enough of living with my mom, so I packed a bag and got on a Greyhound to Houston with my friend Angela. My mom didn't try to stop me. She just sort of gave up. When we got there, we moved into Angela's father's basement. It was beautiful. Angela's dad was a really bad alcoholic, and he always had a half-gallon of Black Velvet. He'd never notice if we drank some. We used to get drunk and videotape each other. I was a hippie at the time, and we used to go over to the park and recite Jim Morrison's poetry, then piss on the concrete. It was so retarded. That's where it all began. We didn't need any other friends. It was me and her and it was our world.

My time in Houston didn't last long, maybe a month. I'm like a target. Everybody's got to fuck with me. One night Angela's dad was all drunk, and he came downstairs and started kissing me and feeling me. I was so scared that I called my mom the next day. I told her what happened, but she wouldn't help me. She was still pissed at me for stealing her boyfriend's booze the night before we left. I knew I wanted out of Houston, so I called this construction worker who I had just met two weeks before I left. He bought my bus ticket back to California.

Once I got back, I got a job at the grocery store. My mom met another guy. He was much older than her and really conservative. He couldn't stand having me around, so my mom paid for me to move in with one of her alcoholic friends in San Rafael.

Everybody in Frisco hated me. That's when I ended up drinking alone and turning into a hard-core alcoholic. The only place that I felt accepted was in Golden Gate Park. There was lots of other hippies, and they had really good drum circles. I met this guy named Jake who started telling me about hopping trains. Jake was awesome. I connected with him instantly. I guess you could say it was love at first sight. We hung out for a while, and then a month later he took me to hop my first train outside the city.

One of the park regulars passes by on 9th Street. She stops and asks Anna if she wants a pair of shoes. Anna declines, but offers thanks:

You really are a Sweet Leif.

Hopping a freight train is a thing of unexplainable beauty. The first train that I hopped was on the fly at probably five miles an hour. The adrenaline was pumping like a fire hydrant. I let the first few cars go by. Then I saw a grainer go by that had my name on it. I was like, I'm getting this bitch. This is my grainer. I ran alongside, grabbed the edge and pulled myself up. It was the biggest rush of my life. All of the sudden you're on this huge piece of metal that could kill you, and you're flying through this beautiful moonlit forest. It's so much better than any other mode of transportation other than actually having wings and being able to fly. Oh my god, the wind! It was magic, the sound of the crossing bells, waving to cars. When I was a baby the only way my mom could get me to sleep was to take me on a ride. It's in my blood. It's like all the fucked up shit from my childhood was erased. Everything I've ever wanted in my life came together in that one moment, and I knew that I wanted to do it forever.

It's so beautiful. You get to see untouched land that nobody ever sees. Not only that, but it makes music. I mean straight-up music. The wheels are turning and everything's tapping and clunking and slamming. It's a song that you can't cover or make money off of. But best of all is that you're doing something that you're not supposed to do. It's my passion.

We jumped off that train in this little hick town and stopped to eat at a missionary. The outside was all brick, and each brick had a signature with a set of railroad tracks. I wrote my name there. It was like, "Yeah I'm a train hopper." While we were eating our food this lady walked by and asked us if we believed in Jesus. I told her not really. She said she'd give us all twenty bucks apiece to pray with her. Blah blah blah, and we got forty bucks.

Have you ever heard of Shotgun Willie? He's this old railroad bull. He's been doing it for years and years, so everybody was worried about him. We went back to the yard and hid behind these tall bushes. All the sudden we saw headlights, and these two huge guys started chasing us. I did this weird ninja somersault down this hill and landed in a bunch of prickers. I was like two feet away from falling into a lake, but my backpack stopped me.

Later that night, we got on another train. The ride north to Oregon is the most beautiful I've ever taken. You're up really high for the whole route over rivers and waterfalls. The colors are beautiful. When I got up to piss, I noticed that there was a dead bird caught in some barbed wire on the other side of the gondola. We wanted to give him another chance to fly, so we threw it off the next trestle and watched it sail for like two hundred feet into the river.

We hadn't bought anything with the forty dollars that the lady had given us, and we were starving. We'd see the signs for restaurants, but we couldn't get off the train. We thought it was going to stop in Eugene, but it went right through. We were so hungry that we jumped off on the fly.

After that, everything went wrong with me and Jake. His mom found out that he had warrants, and she wanted to pay for him to get a flight back to his hometown in Michigan. She wouldn't buy me a ticket, so we decided to separate for a little bit. My mom bought me a ticket back to California, got me an apartment, and then I started working.

There were train tracks right by where I was living. Every time I heard it I would cry. One time I was on the bus to work, and I saw a train stopped on the tracks. I pulled the dinger and ran over to the train and started wiping it with my hands. I took my notebook out of my backpack and smeared the train grease all over it. It was like, this is train grease, and it's sacred. Once I had a taste, I wanted it more than anything. I gave Jake a call, and I told him I wanted to travel with him again. Things had changed, and he said no. You could hear my heart snap.

That night, I threw a huge party in my apartment, and we started knocking down the walls. I still owe three thousand dollars for that. Anyway, I met this guy named Jeremy who always kept this worn out little Yoda action figure in his pocket. He hardly ever said anything, but he was the coolest person I ever met in my life. We became like brothers and sisters. He's here in New York with me now.

In the morning Jeremy, me, and this guy named Stephan hitchhiked out to the same yard where I hopped my first train. I hadn't done it in three months, and I was really nervous. We tried to hop a boxcar on the fly. I was so worried about my hands that I wasn't looking at my feet. When I grabbed the edge, my shoes got caught on something. Everything collided, and I swung under the train to where the wheel was like two feet from my head. I thought I was gonna die. I don't know how it happened, but the next thing I knew I was standing up on the side of the tracks. It must have been some sort of train angel. Ever since then, I won't hop on the fly.

The three of us jumped trains all across the west. We saw a lot of places and met a lot of people. I picked up a stray dog named Rosey in Los Angeles. We were having fun, but what I was really doing was looking for Jake. See, I never allowed myself to love somebody, and for once I did. It was like a hole in my heart. Every destination that I had was in search of him. I went all along the West Coast and through Montana. The one place I knew that I could find him was Tramp Fest. It's a huge gathering of train hoppers down by xxxxx in this field.

I had heard rumors that Jake was fucking this chick named Bobbie. When we got there, I sat down at the fire next to this girl, and I just knew it was her. I said, "You're Bobbie." I asked her where Jake was, and she said that he was in jail for murder. She wouldn't even give me any details, because she said it hurt her too much. This guy was the love of my life, and she had only known him for a couple of weeks. What a bitch.

I don't know what it is, but I'm like a magnet for really fucked up men. I'm terrified of being alone with them. When I was down in New Mexico, I met this Mexican guy, Pablo, who called me gordita, because

I'm fat. Anytime I'd eat, he'd try to take the food away from me. He was such a dick. I don't even know why I let him fuck me. Eventually I got sick of his shit and decided to take off by myself to meet up with some other friends in St. Louis for Halloween.

I was hitchhiking on Route 44 and this guy gave me a ride in a Federal Express truck. At first I sat in the back, then he wanted me to come up front and talk to him. Everything was fine, until he cruised right by my exit. He turned the car around and he said, *(mocks a hillbilly accent)* "You got some beautiful titties." I ran out of the truck and went to a truck stop. I was crying at one of the tables, and one of the waitresses kicked me out. She was such a bitch to do that to another woman.

I went back out to the highway and hitched a ride with these totally retarded people going to a concert. They were all hippies, smoking, drinking. It was really cool, but all the sudden, this one guy tried to touch me. I told him to get his fucking hands off me. He said, *(hillbilly accent)* "I can touch you if I want. We're giving you a ride." Then the other guy started touching me. I flipped out and just started punching them in the head like thirty times. They dropped me off at the next exit.

When I got to St. Louis, I was all by myself. My friends had already left town, because it was after Halloween. I hung out and got drunk every night. One night I was wasted and I passed out. When the cops woke me up, I couldn't find my dog. I threw a fit, so they let me go find her. I eventually found her with these two crazy guys. They were drinking a half-gallon of vodka and a half-gallon of tequila. They gave me a few drinks, then it started raining, so we went underneath an underpass. They were really nice, and they made me a little bed on the cement.

When I woke up, there were four hands all over me. I started screaming and throwing fists. They were like, *(hillbilly accent)* "You know you want it," and they were trying to take my clothes off. Then they started to get worried I was going to tell somebody. They were whispering, and I heard them say they were gonna kill me. That scared the shit out of me. I stuffed most of my shit in my bag and took off running. Rosey didn't follow. I called and called, but she wouldn't come. When she finally did, I hit her. That's the only time I ever hit my dog, and I feel horrible about it. When I look back, I think those two guys were holding her. I lost a lot of shit. I was keeping a journal of each city, and that was gone. I didn't even have a jacket.

I walked the streets for a few days, then I bumped into Pablo from Mexico and some of his friends. I was still pissed at him, but it was good to see a familiar face. We ended up staying in a warehouse and he said,

photo Monte

"Come mere fat ass bitch. Fuck me." I freaked out and started slamming my head into the wall. I was screaming all sorts of gibberish—a total breakdown. That went on for like an hour, and then I was just shaking in the corner. Pablo got on top of me and said I was making him horny. I punched him in the head and he ran off.

Right when I was leaving St. Louis, I ended up meeting this guy named Reggie who told me I was the most beautiful girl he'd ever met. We rode in the back of a U Haul all the way to Key West, and then we left to meet up with Jeremy and his friends in Charleston and then go to New York. On the way there, we stopped in some hick town in Georgia to see some of Reggie's friends. He said he only wanted to stay for one day, but that turned into two weeks.

Reggie's friends were stuck-up yuppies with nine-to-fives. They were trying to get him away from the traveling lifestyle. One of them had a two-bedroom apartment, and he said that Reggie could stay there until he got on his feet. It sucked, because I wanted to meet up with my friends.

Reggie was a different person around his friends. He was always finding hot chicks on his friend's computer and showing them to me. It was like he wanted to prove that he could treat me like shit and I'd still stick around. Eventually, I told him that things weren't going to work out. He was cool about it and promised me that no matter what he was going to help me get to my friends.

That night, we went out to the highway and tried to hitch north. We didn't get a ride, so we spent the night in a ditch. He told me that he loved me and wanted to be with me more than anything, and he'd take me all the way to New York if he had to. When I woke up, he was gone. I haven't spoken to him since then. He didn't even email me. The next day, I got a ride to Charleston, but my friends had left. My next ride was to Trenton. From there, I spanged *(spare changed)* money for a train ticket to New York. I had to buy a pair of sunglasses and find this guy to pretend he was blind so they'd let me take Rosey. I met up with my friends two days ago in Tompkins Square. I should be happy, but I'm not.

I'm fucking pregnant from Reggie. Evil fucker. He left me by the side of the highway and he doesn't even know if I'm alive. We always used condoms, but two times they broke. I haven't had my period in two months. I've been puking all the time. I feel it. I have a baby. Why can't it be him that got pregnant? He's the one that left me. He doesn't even know that he did it. Even if he did, he wouldn't care.

I can't have this kid. If I have this kid it's going to come out mentally retarded. I drink everyday. One of my friends calls me a baby killer because I don't want to have it. I know what I have to do, but that costs money, a lot, like two to four hundred dollars. I never even really believed in abortion. All of the sudden, I've got to find a way to get all this money, deal with this pain, and I'm not going to have any support.

Anna's roller skating proficiency has dwindled significantly with two additional beers. I have to hold her by the hand as we skitter over the pedestrian bridge to East River Park. There's a group of about five people sitting around one of the picnic tables. Two of them are cooking up heroin. Anna introduces me to her dog, and then goes to sleep.

Anna left town a week later. I've gotten one email from her. She said that she's doing OK and living indoors back in San Francisco. Justifiably, she left many of my questions unanswered.

Gypsy
New York, New York 1978
compugoth@yahoo.com

Gypsy is an extremely withdrawn individual. Amid the feverish ranting of Crusty Lane he's content to sit off to the side with silent, stoic composure. He accepts my offer for an interview with mellow indifference and rolls out brief, unde-tailed responses in a restrained, melancholy droll. I spend almost as much time asking questions as he does answering.

I grew up in a two-bedroom apartment on 96th Street with an older brother and sister. My dad was a cop, and my mom was a waitress. My parents worked a lot, so I didn't see them very much. We always worried that my dad would get shot.

When my parents were home, they talked to me a lot about meditation and making the right choices. Their biggest thing was that I had to do good in school. They wanted me to be a doctor or a lawyer or something respectable in society. They were really into family values, and they demanded that I give them respect. Whatever they said was the last word. You couldn't answer back. They were very strict about the things that I could do and who I was allowed to hang out with. Every day after school, I had to be home at three o'clock. If I got bad grades, they'd smack me around a bit, not too bad, but enough where it hurt. I guess it was a pretty stable house, but my parents still fought a lot about money.

I was a quiet kid. I guess it was hard for me to inter-act with other people, because I didn't really talk to anyone outside my family. Going to school was a pretty difficult thing. There were a lot of rich white kids there, and they used to make fun of me because I was Indian.

I remember this Italian kid, Joe Rizzo, who used to yell shit at me from in front of the school door. He'd call me the red dot special, or say that I worshiped cows. For a while I was scared to do anything, but then I started fighting back. I got in a lot of fights.

School was the first time I really realized I was different from other kids. See, my parents didn't practice Hinduism or anything. We ate meat. We did have something called the Festival of Lights, but that was only once a year. In school I was the only Indian person around. Every day people would ask me questions about being Indian. I had to learn more about it just to answer their questions. Sometimes I got scared, because I didn't know what to say. After a while it got annoying. I don't like it when people ask me questions about being Indian.

Sorry.

My teachers always treated me differently. I had pretty good grades, like A's and B's, but they were always harder on me. Like if I got problems wrong on my homework, I'd be the only one who they'd make redo it. I didn't have any friends until I got to middle school. There was this kid Matt who was like a metal head. He got picked on too. We used to skip out of classes and go hang out in the bathroom. One day, he sparked up a joint and asked me if I wanted some. He was my friend, so I said OK. It was strange. *(wispy giggle)* I was laughing so much I didn't know what to do. I couldn't do school work or anything like that. I loved it. It was stimulating. It got my mind off the school kids, and I got to relax.

When I realized that more kids in school smoked, I started to have friends for the first time in my life. Smoking pot was like an escape into a fantasy world. I could be all the things that I wasn't at home. I remember watching *Easy Rider* for the first time, and right away I wanted to get a motorcycle and run away. That was my dream. I thought smoking pot was the best thing that ever happened to me.

Pretty soon, I started smoking every day. My grades started falling a little bit, and my dad was really mad. I never told people that my dad was a cop. It was weird. It was a bad thing to be. Everybody was against cops. He always told me stories about little kids who he busted for drugs. I was so angry at my father for keeping me inside the apartment that it only encouraged me to go out and smoke more.

When I was fifteen, things were getting worse at home. I was trapped—totally bored. I still had to be home right after school. One day I decided that I didn't want to go back, so I stayed out all night and fell asleep on the train. In the morning, I went back to school. When I found out that my parents called the office, I walked out.

I stayed at some of my friends' houses for a few nights, and they introduced me to these older guys. I guess you could say they were hippies. I stayed with them for a few weeks and partied. I didn't go to school or anything. It was a great time, but after a while, I kind of felt like I was a burden on these people. I couldn't deal with going back to my parents' apartment, so I went to this place called Covenant House. It's like a shelter for kids.

I showed up and told them my story, and they said I could stay. It was kind of scary living there, but I had my own room. They had rules about cleaning the place. They also did drug testing, but you'd just have somebody else piss in the cup. The curfew there was ten o'clock, so that was much better than my parents' house.

My friends at Covenant House were like brothers.

My parents were all crying and stuff when they came to see me. We were all screaming at each other. They said I was going to wind up on drugs and in jail. Then they tried to tell me that they were going to get a lawyer and take me home, but I knew they couldn't do that. There was no way I was going to go back with them. I still stayed in touch with my brother, and sometimes I'd go visit on weekends. It was cool in a sense, but I just couldn't deal with being there all the time.

Covenant House let you do whatever you wanted as long as you didn't miss the curfew. The counselors gave you like a ten-dollar-a-week allowance, and I could make some extra cash by helping people hook up with weed. Me and my friends went to a lot of concerts and hung out with the punk kids. My favorite place was Tompkins Square Park. There were all kinds of people. You saw people with mohawks and piercings and tattoos sleeping on the grass everywhere. It was really laid back, do whatever you want to do. I was like wow.

I did pretty good in CDS High School with A's and B's. Leaving home really made me do better in school, because I had less to worry about. I had my own thing going, and people wouldn't pick on me. At first I wouldn't tell anybody where I lived, but after a while, I got mad and just told all my friends that I lived at Covenant House. They were cool with it. I actually got more respect, because I was taking control of my own life.

I stayed in Covenant House even after I graduated high school. My first job was working as a bar tender at a place called Downtown Beirut. They never really asked me for my age, so it worked out really good. Everybody in the whole rock and roll scene would be there—Debby Harry, punk people, bikers.

Everything was like the motorcycle movies—not one person in a suit and tie. It was a good time for me. I worked there until they closed it in '96.

When I was twenty-one years old I decided I wanted to travel. I was over eighteen, so I knew that if I left the house, I couldn't come back. I talked to the counselors, and we left on good terms. Then I jumped on a bus to San Francisco with some of my friends. It was wild and scary. I thought it was going to be like New York, but I didn't know anybody. Everything was way more expensive. My friends left after a week, but I stayed for another month.

I really wanted to get back to New York, but I didn't have any money. One day I was spare changing, and this guy said he'd give me a hundred dollars if I jerked off in front of him. I wasn't happy about it, but that was the only way I could buy a bus ticket. It was scary. I don't think I could do it again.

When I got back to New York, I tried getting work, but a lot of the clubs had closed. My friends took turns letting me stay in their apartments. I was still in touch with my family, but I didn't want to go there. Eventually I ended up staying at a squat downtown. There was about twenty people in there. We fixed it up and partied a lot. The only drug that we allowed was pot. We kicked out the people who had hard drugs. One night my friends brought back these chicks from Jersey. They were acting all chi chi and they wanted to leave, but one of the guys wouldn't let them out. That brought the cops, and the squat got shut down.

In May of '99 I ended up out on the streets. I lost my bags and my phone numbers, so I didn't have anybody to call. I just hung out around Washington Square Park. A lot of guys would try to hit on me. They'd get you drunk and try to take you home. A lot of my friends pulled tricks just so they could get some money to get a hotel. I try to stay away from that.

That summer, I ran into an old friend who had a spare room in his place. I stayed there for a year. Every day I'd get stoned and go panhandle. Six months ago they had to move, and I couldn't get enough money together to get a place, so I've just been living out here.

I know a lot of these kids, but a lot of them left at the end of the summer. A lot of them are into dope, but I just smoke and drink. I try to avoid the conflicts, but sometimes it's impossible. A few days ago, these kids down by the river were saying things about the way I look, and they way I dress. They said I should go home to mommy and daddy. We started fighting, and that's how I got this scab on my face.

I don't really know what I'm going to do with my future. I went to the library and checked out all of these things about schools, but I need to get an address to send out applications. I'm pretty sick of staying out here, and I want to get on with my life. At first I thought that it would be an adventure living out here, because I'd have my freedom, but now the reality is seeping in. I know that if I stay out here any longer it's going to kill me.

I speak with Gypsy on St. Marks Place again in November. He tells me that he's not interested in completing a follow up interview, and he adamantly refuses to let me photograph him. I pass him several times on the street in the winter, but we don't stop to talk. More than a year after our interview, he approaches me on Crusty Lane. I'm surprised that he remembers my name. When I hand him the manuscript, he eagerly pages to his section. After he finishes reading, he tells me that he wants his real name and picture included.

Stephanie
Los Angeles, California 1980
twatrot666@hotmail.com

I first meet Stephanie and Bolt as I'm riding my bike through East River Park late one night in October 2001. I nod a tentative hello as I pass, but the foreboding presence of Bolt and Anubis the pitbull are an unnerving deterrent. After I peddle a few hundred feet, I circle back and arrange an interview. When we reach the river, I ask if the couple if they would be comfortable talking in front of each other. Stephanie replies that it's no trouble at all. They're married.

Stephanie takes the first interview. At first Bolt eyes me cautiously, but after a few minutes he seems satisfied that I'm harmless and curls up on the concrete with Anubis. Stephanie responds to my questions confidently, with elevated Californian inflection.

My mom's really cool. She's this punk rocker chick,* really fucking cool, smokes weed, drinks beer, snorts coke—really cool person. My dad was like this stuck-up asshole who doesn't even drink, smoke, nothing—typical Indian from New Delhi. I lived with both of them in East Los Angeles until they got divorced when I was two. When my mom split for Tennessee, my dad couldn't handle us, so he bounced us around to different relatives. I grew up in Santa Ana, Hollywood, Irvine, Tustin, Costa Mesa—all over.

All the relatives on my dad's side were straight and narrow Indian assholes. They took me to their churches and tried to discipline us. I liked it much better staying with my mom's people. Her family was

---

*Upon examining the rough draft, Stephanie asked me to change "punk rocker" to "butt rocker," then prompted by the suggestion of a friend, she chose the word, "Hessian" because "We're white trash, not city folk."

crazy, and I could do what ever I wanted. My uncle Allen and his son are in Quentin for selling coke and boosting VCRs. That was a cool family.

Me and my sister did a lot of things kids do, like nigger knocking and shit. You know, knock and run? We'd shoot BB's at people's dogs and play Atari. There wasn't much consistency with everybody else, but me and my sister were always together. She was my best friend in the world. We always found ways to amuse ourselves. I remember one time we were at my grandmother's house, and we stole her cigarettes and went under the porch. It took us a whole book of matches before we got one lit, then my sister ran around yelling that she had cancer. We were basically just delinquent little hood rats.

Nobody could get us into a normal routine. One of my aunts tried for a while, but I can't remember her name, maybe Rahim or Pudgee. She'd try to make us do our homework and not let us watch scary movies. But that didn't work out. We were too wild.

I loved school. I loved breakfast, and I loved lunch. We hardly ever really got fed at home. School lunch was the shit, pancakes, Pop Tarts. That's the only thing I liked about school. What sucked was you had to carry this little card, so everybody knew you were poor. I used to get in fights over that a lot. I did all right as far as grades. I wouldn't study, but I could pass a test.

When I was like seven, my mom decided she wanted custody of us. She was working at a La-Z-Boy factory in Tennessee and was living in her own trailer. My dad gave us up right away, because he wasn't taking care of us anyway. Mom sent us a letter with plane tickets, and she said that she had a surprise for us when we got there. It was kind of weird in the airport, because I didn't really remember what my mom looked like. But when I saw her it was like immaculate acception. Like, "That's my mom."

Mom took us back to the trailer and showed us the surprise. It was this huge broken ass boat in the backyard. It was cool to play in it. My sister and I used to listen to Cindy Lauper and pretend we were going somewhere. After a while it filled up with beer cans, and we couldn't play in there anymore.

The first two years in Tennessee were awesome. My mom had remarried, and they had a kid. There were also four other stepbrothers. My step dad was pretty nice at first. He was an ex con who had all the boys over playing poker, smoking weed. He was in jail a lot and was gone most of the time. The rest of the time he worked the night shift in some lumber factory or something. I liked him, because he didn't bother me. He didn't get on my case when my sister and me pinched his stash.

First time I smoked a joint I got so high that I could just hear my heart going bup, bup, bup. I went into my bedroom, and that Prince song "Purple Rain" came on. I turned the lights off, and I just melted. It was soooo fucking cool.

School in Tennessee was different than LA. In LA nobody really gave a shit that I was half Indian, because I looked Mexican. When I moved to Tennessee, I was the only person of color in the school. Little kids would call me nigger and shit, and I'd get really pissed off. On top of that, they still made fun of us for being poor. We were so poor that we only had three spoons in the house. We had to wait to eat.

My mom cheated on my step dad a lot. He drank all the time, and he was always passed out in stupors. My mom told him that if he stopped drinking, she'd get back with him. He did. That's when he became the big ass dickhead from hell. See when he was drunk, we got to do anything we wanted, like camp out in the backyard with tents and stuff. After he got sober, he started coming home every day at exactly three o'clock. As soon as he got home, that's when the yelling started. "Wraah! Wraah! What are you doing? Where's dinner?" My stepfather's still sober to this day, and he's still a dick.

He smacked us around a lot. One time, my mom drove off in the car, and my dad went after her. I wanted to see what was going on, so I left the baby with our neighbor Vern. When he came back, my step dad started screaming that Vern was a child molester and ran over there and grabbed the baby. Then he smacked me with a two by four. He'd hit us with belts before, but that was the first time that I got hit really hard.

I was the oldest in the house, so I had a lot of responsibilities. I always had to stay home and watch the kids. That sucked, because we didn't even have a telephone. My parents wouldn't let me join the soft-ball team, because they thought it would interfere with my baby-sitting. I used to pretend that I missed the bus so I could go to practice, but that didn't work out for long. At night, I'd sneak out. I didn't even go get high or anything. I just wanted to see my friends. One time I went to the YMCA to do gymnastics. When I got back the lights went on, and there was my step dad. He kept me hostage all night hitting me with this cane, talking all kinds of stupid shit. He told me that I had to go back to LA. They had threatened to do that before, but I didn't care. It actually made me act worse. The only bad thing was that I'd be away from my sister.

When I went back to LA, I moved in with my uncle in Los Nietos. He was really neglectful, so that was cool. I had my own apartment. I slept in the living room and my grandfather was in the bedroom. He was really sick, so I had to change his bladder bag and feed him. My uncle paid me a hundred dollars a week to take care of him.

There were a lot of other kids around, and I had a boyfriend named Carlos. He was this little cholo *(gangster)* and his older brothers were Serranyos. He always had his hair slicked back and creased pants, looked just like Ralph Macchio. Ralph Macchio was the shit. I lost my virginity to Carlos, and it was cool.

At Whittier High School I hung out with a pretty hardcore group of cholos, and they respected me. Have you ever seen *Blood in Blood Out*? It's this cholo movie about drugs and shit. That's what my life was like. My friends all had low riders, and they rolled with different gangs. It was a lot of excitement. Then one of my friends got caught with a brick of weed, and I was holding his gun for him. The school pressed charges and we got kicked out.

The whole time I was in Los Nietos, my dad kept saying that he wanted me to move in with him, but he really didn't mean it. My step mom just kept on nagging him, saying that he had a responsibility to take care of his own blood. I really didn't remember my father other than a vague image. I guess I missed the thought of having a dad, but I didn't miss him as a person. When the shit went down with the gun, my father called and said he was going to take me in.

I was scared to be leaving, kind of wary, like a dog. It was weird when he pulled up. He looked like this weird hunchbacked dude with his pants pulled up to his waist and these big glasses. He looked Mexican, but he had this thick Indian accent.

Alisa Viejo was total Southern California suburbs. I was fourteen, so it was my second year in high school. The place was filled with totally snotty 90210 people, trendy fucking yuppie kids. At first I fit in with the popular clique, but after a while that got boring, so I started hanging with these four anarchist, fuck you, freaky freaky, 666 kind of kids.

One time they took me to a graveyard, and we got into all this philosophy. Then one kid whipped out a Satanic Bible. It's all about enduring in carnal pleasures and not having a hand that powers over you. Do unto others as they do unto you, not turn the other cheek. It's all about doing your own thing. We'd draw a pentagram in the dirt and hold hands and maybe chant a backwards prayer, but mostly we just hung out in cemeteries and talked. We didn't sacrifice babies or anything.

At first, I was into it for the shock value. It scared people. But then I'd go home and listen to some punk, and I'd feel the blankets on my bed getting tighter. Or, if I lost something in my room, I'd pray to Satan and I'd find it. I was like, oh, this shit really works. Pretty soon I started dressing really punk and wearing a smiley.* That kind of freaked out the trendy kids in school. I kind of liked that, so I shaved my head into bi hawks. My dad totally freaked. He called me a cholo. He doesn't know anything about anything. He's Indian. After that, I pierced my nose in the school bathroom.

I guess it was a cry for attention. I've seriously never hugged my dad, no affection whatsoever. All

---

*A smiley is a metal chain held together with a pad lock. It serves the dual purpose of jewelry and weapon.

they wanted me to do was study to be a doctor or lawyer or whatever. Anytime I went out, they had to meet the person. I lied a lot.

I spent a lot of time at this place called Cafe Lo Lo. A lot of gothic kids hung out there. They were cool, because they weren't affiliated with any kind of authority figures, and they did a lot of drugs. One of my best friends was this big chick who sold dope, named Cathy. She was always sleeping, nodded out. We would lug her around the school from class to class. I didn't know what was wrong with her. I just thought she was a fat chick, so she slept a lot. One night we were sitting around at her house drinking tequila and she shot up. I asked her what it was like, and she gave me the basic *Train Spotting* description—a thousand tongues licking her. She didn't want to give it to me, but I was like, "Kick down, motherfucker!" I was so drunk I didn't even feel it. After a while, I started going to her house a lot and shooting up and nodding out in front of the television. It was hella cool.

Around that time, I started cutting myself. When I got mad, I'd go into my room and take out this cool gothic dagger and slice my arms. It really released a lot of anger. Sometimes I'd get rigs and start withdrawing blood. About a week before Christmas, my grandfather in Los Nietos passed away. I was really upset. All of my father's relatives came together for a reunion at our house. They were really mad at my dad, because he didn't tell any of them that Grandpa was about to die. They got into a big argument, and I went into my room and started cutting myself. My dad busted in and dragged me down in front of everybody yelling that I was crazy. After that, they stuck me in rehab.

They kept putting me in different facilities, and each time I'd bust out. My parents would file a missing person report, but when the cops brought me back, my dad would kick me out again. I had nowhere to go, so I started squatting at different beaches and breaking into trailers in Treasure Island. I tried to go to school for a while, because that's where my friends were, but there weren't any buses from where I was staying. I hitchhiked for a while with some beaners and truck drivers, but that was too complicated, so I just said fuck it and dropped out.

After a few weeks, the cops picked me up, and I got sent to a hardcore inpatient rehab. They put me on all these psych meds that made me more fucking crazy—Zoloft, Kigente, Paxil. I had to take three in the morning and two at night. There wasn't any sensation. I was just tired and numb. It made me really sensitive to the sun, so I had to wear sunglasses all the time. As soon as I got out of there, I bought a bag of pot and went to my parents' house.

My parents weren't home, so I had to break a window to get in. I got some clothes, then I broke some more windows and left. The next day I went out to the freeway to hitchhike up to Berkeley. The first car to stop was this little Toyota Van filled with kids headed all the way to Frisco. They were like a combination of hippies and punk rockers. They really dug the tapes that I had and they liked me, so they let me move into their place in San Fran. They were all broke ass motherfuckers except for this one kid who was like a trust-fund kid or something.

After a few weeks I met this kid named Brian. He was kind of seedy, but we clicked. I moved in with him. Then he ended up getting me pregnant against my will.

So it was rape?

In a sense, but I won't say it was.

But it was penetration without your consent?

Right. I went to the clinic and Medicaid paid for an abortion. It fucked up my head really bad for a long time. I ended up leaving Brian and moved back with the original kids. I went to court and got emancipated from my parents, then I got a job with this place called Youth Industry. They hired me when I was like sixteen as a bicycle mechanic. For about a year I was kind of keeping it together and paying rent, but the people at the house were shooting a lot of dope, so I ended up getting hooked on heroin. Before, dope was just a once in a while thing, but there I was exposed to it every day. I started getting kind of scandalous and stealing people's bags.

It didn't take long for me to lose my job and be totally broke. One day I went down the street to a methadone clinic, and they dosed me that day. I went back into the house and went into the kitchen and made a peanut butter and jelly sandwich. Everybody else was dope sick, so they thought that was kind of weird. For a while, the methadone held me, but once I got on maintenance, it wasn't enough. I started taking Quanadines, Zanex bars, and some codeine, then I'd dose the methadone and take a cup of coffee, so it would all kick in. After that I'd try to score some dope. I was doing anything I could get my hands on.

My life was totally in the junkie bubble. There was a TV and a VCR. I watched a lot of *Drug Store Cowboy*, *Naked Lunch*, shit like that. About a year later, I went to the library and looked at what books I owed: *Zodiac Killer* and *Junkie*. I don't even remember taking them out. Everything was revolving around being a junkie.

On Halloween I stole these two guitars from this dude's house, and I was gonna sell 'em. I stepped into this McDonald's bathroom on Powell and there was this black crackhead chick who gave me some heroin and some crack. I don't know why, I guess she was just crazy. Anyway, this security guard started yelling that we had to come out. I took like another minute, and he came back in and started screaming at me. Then he took the two guitars and smashed them against the wall. I was like, "You fucking stupid nigger motherfucker. Fuck you!" I grabbed what was left of the guitar, and I started bashing him. I think I got him pretty good. Two of the windows got smashed, and pretty soon the cops were there arresting me. I had like forty Clonapins in my pocket and I was crushing them up in the car, but they got me with a tenth of heroin and a solid of crack.

After a week in the lockup, I was back out on the street. They let me out on OR *(own recognizance)*. You just pretty much promise that you're going to court. It was about then that I started selling some serious crack, like twenty packages a day. That would be like five dimes, or ten nickels. There was a lot of cash, but I was mostly shooting it away. I also smoked a lot of crack. Before my court date came, they got me with five dimes.

They put me in 850 Bryant *(jail)*. I was in D pod, the sick tank. The whole place was covered with mats. There weren't any bunks, because they didn't want you to fall out. There was eight other women in there—mostly hardcore prison bitches, but there were about three people who I already knew from the street. They had us on a methadone program and the methadone guy, we called him the dope man, came by with this little cart twice a day. Once he left his cart right outside the cell and walked away for like a minute. There was about a foot of space underneath our cell door, so I reached through and grabbed fifteen bottles of methadone. When the dope man came back, he just wheeled the cart away. No guards ever came or anything. Maybe the guy was scared that he'd lose his job.

I called a big huddle in the cell, and I started passing out the bottles. Some of us were drinking like three bottles each, then we'd flush 'em down the toilet. I shoved one up my fucking cunt and then another. They're like big round bottles, two hundred milligrams, so it really hurt. Other people did it too. For like two days, everyone was feeling nice. I still had one bottle left when they moved me to G tank. I fell off my bunk twice I was nodding so hard. That was the coolest pick I ever had in jail. I got all this respect from the other inmates. If I ever had to go to prison after this I'd be automatically accepted, because they'd put in a good word for me right off the yard that I was a down ass bitch. Jail's like that. It's all about not backing down from anything.

I got bounced in and out of jail about three times. I don't even really know how long I was in there, because when you're on a methadone program, you spend a lot of time just nodding out. The second time, they wouldn't release me on OR, so I had to go out on SPR *(supervised pretrial release)*. I checked in for a while, but then I stopped.

One day I was walking through Golden Gate Park, and I had like two shots already cooked up in my bra for my wakeup. Somebody said there were narcs rolling through the park, but I didn't think anything of it. Two guys jumped right out and said, "I see you missed your court date, Stephanie." They knew my name and everything. That time I was in for like four months. They wouldn't let me out at all. You only get two chances.

After the four months, they gave me the opportunity to go to a rehab center for a year instead of doing the rest of my sentence. Of course I took it. It was called Walden House. No methadone, and you couldn't leave. I wanted to run a couple times, but I knew I couldn't. I was totally depressed. Seriously, people who knew me before I went to rehab told me that the rehab was really killing me. It was like mind control.

There were three cardinal rules: No drugs, no violence, no having sex. If you did that, you went to jail. Actually, you could have sex if you had a boyfriend on the outside, but you had to apply for a visit. If you fucked up in any small way, they'd take you in this little room and just yell at you. Like, "You're a piece of shit! You come in here, and you shit all over us, and that's why you're a fucking junkie! Pull yourself up!" It's called the Bench. One time I got put on lockdown for stealing a candy bar. I was laughing at 'em the whole time they were screaming at me. I was always in trouble, always scheming something.

All the other rehabs were like soft like, "Lets talk about your feelings." This one was hardcore. They had intercoms in your room that woke you up at seven o'clock. I cooked and cleaned nine to five. You had to ask if you wanted to go to the fucking bathroom. It was almost impossible to get high. I did it like twice, and I got put on lockdown for like a month each time. It beat the shit out of me.

After seven months I was working in the kitchen, and this dude kept throwing water at me. At first I was laughing, but then he wouldn't stop. I took this coffee creamer and threw it all over him. He dragged me from the dining room to the kitchen. I got up and just started beating the dog shit out of him, kicking him in the face. When I stopped, I just ran up to my room and started packing my bags, because I knew I was going to get kicked out. I was scared I'd have to go back to jail, but they ended up letting me graduate. I think they were scared that I could sue them for letting me get assaulted.

I was twenty-one when I got out of Walden House. The second day I got high. Then I talked to my probation officer, and she said that I had to go to a halfway house for secondary treatment. They put me in another program called Grer House. You lived there, but they let you leave for work. It was really cool. The fist day I got there I slept in till noon. It was awesome. I had a job working at a restaurant, and I had access to all my money. As long as I followed the house rules, I could go out any time I wanted. We did get drug tested, so I had to stay clean.

On my free time I met these kids and we started a band. I played drums. Eventually, I started going to bars and doing a lot of drinking, because alcohol wouldn't show up in a test. I was never really an alcoholic—it was just taking the place of the heroin. Grer House was so lax, they had no idea what was going on. Even when I kept on showing up late, they just gave me warnings. That's when I met Bolt.

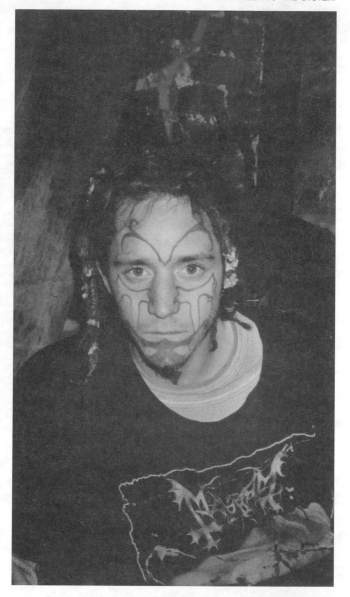

Bolt
New York, New York

It's all about shock value. I could be walking down 42nd Street at rush hour, and people will part like the Red Sea. I love it. Sometimes old ladies will look at my face and scream. I scream back. Stephanie hates it when I do that.

It's two o'clock in the morning when I finish talking to Stephanie. She gently rubs Bolt's shoulder and rouses him from his sidewalk slumber. The couple switches places as Anubis climbs on the bench. Bolt's hands tremble as he rolls a loose tobacco cigarette.

At first Bolt appears disoriented, but gradually he settles into a steady hypnotic tone. His voice swoops in pitch as he alternates between rapid-fire recollection and calm introspective analysis. Although I find it difficult to digest some of the details of Bolt's narrative, I am captivated by his energy.

I was born in Bellevue. I have no idea who my dad was. It was just me and my mom for a long time. She was kinda tall and skinny, really pale, changed her hair a lot. I don't know what color her real hair was. She was usually pretty calm and quiet, unless somebody was paying her to do otherwise. She was a prostitute.

We moved around a lot. I remember parts of Brooklyn. I remember Queens, Uptown, down here. We hopped around a lot of hotel rooms and different guys' houses. Sometimes she'd pull her tricks with me in the room. She'd just tell me to watch the TV while guys came and went. I watched it so much I thought Archie Bunker was my dad. On TV I noticed a lot of kids had a mom and a dad and lived in the same place every night. They were always happy and laughy. For me it wasn't like that. I always knew something was wrong.

I used to get nightmares from watching my mom shoot dope. It looked like it hurt. She'd start talking all slow about things I didn't understand, and then she'd fall asleep. She gave me food, but I don't think I really loved her. I always used to get mad because I never had anything I wanted. The one thing that I wanted the most was army guys—all the kids on TV had army guys. I remember one time I was at the playground, and I picked up this other kid's army guy and I wouldn't let it go. The kid started crying and my mom dragged me away screaming, but it was all right because I got to keep him. I still have him today. A few months later when I turned six, my mom left me in this room for two days with just the TV. When she came back she had this box full of old busted toys. That was kinda cool.

I had a lot of imaginary friends, but they only came out when nobody else was around. I liked talking to the TV. It was like my friend for a while. I guess my first hero was Tanto. He was cool, because he didn't talk. He just hung out. I didn't really understand that it was fiction. I thought that people lived in there. One day I got in a lot of trouble, because I found a hammer, and I broke the TV trying to set the people free.

When I was seven, my mother put me in PS 62. That was her way of getting rid of me for a while. I freaked out, because I'd never seen that many kids before. I didn't know what to make of the classroom. I didn't want to learn how to write or anything. They gave me a pencil, and I thought it was a toy, so I stuffed it down my pants. They found it, because I stabbed myself in the knee. For the fist two months, I didn't talk to any of the other kids at all. Then I saw this kid who had dirty clothes like me. We started hanging out, because we were the only kids who never had a lunch. We used to fight each other every day, but then we were best friends. After summer vacation I never saw that kid again. I looked for him in the fall, and I was mad that he wasn't there.

In first grade I was so scared of school that I just kept really really quiet. But being there a second year I turned into a loud motherfucker. I was running around everywhere. The second week they put me in a classroom with just a few other kids. That sucked, because they were retarded. One kid had this funky metal thing on his head. That scared the shit out me. The kid who sat next to me was a big fat kid who always drooled on himself, and the teacher was this big ugly Halloween-looking bitch. I'd just go to sleep and try not to think about the kid with the metal thing. *(laughs)*

My mom never brought me back for third grade. She'd just leave me in playgrounds for hours. I thought that was the greatest thing — beat sitting in the hotel room. If she put me on the jungle gym I could only play on the jungle gym. If I fell off, I'd have to get back on real quick, or when she came back she'd beat the shit out of me.

To this day, I still hate the corner of Houston and Avenue A. There used to be a candy store there. When I was nine years old, my mother took me there, gave me five bucks, and told me that she'd be back in a little while. I thought it was great. I ate candy for hours, then I sat outside the store waiting for her to come back. I waited and waited for hours. I was cold as fuck, I had a huge stomachache, and I was scared as fuck.

At like four in the morning, a bunch of punk rockers walked by—scared the shit out of me. See, I knew the difference between normal people and punk rockers. They scared me shitless with their bright colors and funny hair. There was this one lady who had this huge pink mohawk and metal chains hanging all over her. Her name was Ice. She asked me what I was doing there, and I said I was waiting for my mom. Ice sat there talking with me for hours. When the sun came up she told me that my mother wasn't coming back. I was bawling. That morning Ice took me home with her. I fell asleep right there in her arms. That was like the first time I ever slept with my arms around somebody.

When I woke up I was in this huge room with a few other punk rockers in it. There were candles all over the place and holes in the wall. The smell was kind of funky. Later I found out that it was a squat called Dos Blockos, the original See Squat.* (But don't say that I lived in See Squat, because See Squat now is full of idiots. I've got more right to be there than any of them.)

Ice kind of became my mom. It was awesome, because I could do anything I wanted whenever I wanted. The only thing I had to do was to pick up the garbage. That was really no big deal, because the beer cans were toys. For a while, Ice kept me away from all the other people, and I'd only hang out in her room. The people who came to visit all did the same thing as my mom—shot heroin. I didn't really know what it was. I just thought that was something moms did. One time, and this is really fucked up, she poked me with a needle, and I cried. Then I felt really funny, like sleepy. When I woke up it was like a weird dream, but my arm still hurt. I didn't know what to make of it. Ice never did that to me again.

I lost my fear of punk rocker people pretty quick. Now I thought that all the normal looking people

---

*One of the few remaining large-scale squats in the Lower East Side.

were scary. Gradually, I got to know the squatters. They were all in their late teens, early twenties. Ice was eighteen when she picked me up. I really didn't have any friends my own age, but Ice had a boyfriend. We'd hang out, and he'd put me on his shoulders and run around the room and I felt like a kid.

When I started getting more comfortable, I turned into a real pain in the ass. I was a real high-energy kid. If you left your stuff laying around, I'd pick it up and start playing with it. I was always trying to run up and jump into girls' laps. If they tried to kiss their boyfriend, I'd get in his way. I'd fuck with all the guys, because I was too little for them to beat me up. The squatters gave me the name Unwanted. For ten more years it stuck.

I could do pretty much whatever I wanted inside the squat, but Ice was really worried about letting me out on the street alone. Pedophiles would always try to pick me up. It got to the point where I was leery of everybody I didn't know. If I didn't know you, you couldn't get me to budge. I thought everybody was out to hurt me.

After I stayed in Dos Blockos for a year, we went to Chicago for a few weeks. Some friends of Ice drove us there in a van. That was a big thing for me, because I thought everything was city all around the world. It was the first time I got to see forests and fields and wilderness. It was amazing. Once we got to Chicago it was pretty scary—a lot of black people. We stayed at another squat and Ice and her friends did some drugs. Eventually some people got arrested, and we drove back to New York. I learned a little about the world from that. I learned that people sucked everywhere, not just here.

Ice tried to bring me back to school once when I

was eleven. I had kind of a little punk rock look, because all the people in the squat would spike my hair and rip my shirts. When they put me in the classroom, nobody would talk to me. That kind of pissed me off, so the first day I got into a fight, and I beat this kid up really bad. The principal said he was going to call my mom. I remembered Ice telling me that if they said they were calling your mom, run away. That's what I did. I busted out of the school and kept running all over the city. I thought that every grown-up was out to get me. Finally, I ran into a couple kids who I knew from the squat, and they brought me back home.

The next few days were pretty intense for Ice. She was starting to get scared that she could get in a lot of trouble for keeping me in Dos Blockos. She was really nervous, shaking, always looking out the window. If she heard a loud noise, she'd freak out. A couple times she told me to hide under the couch. After three days, she sat me down and we had a talk. She said that she was going to take me to see a man, and I had to tell him that my mommy left me.

When we got to Social Services, Ice gave me a big hug and she was crying. She waited a few blocks away and told me to walk up to the door. The guy at the front desk was an asshole. I just walked out. Ice waited until I got a few blocks away, and then she ran up and gave me a big hug. That was really cool. I'll never forget that day. That night, we went back to Dos Blockos just as if nothing ever happened.

I told Ice everything. She knew more about me than I did. She was much better than my first mom, and I didn't want to give her up. I knew that my living situation wasn't normal, but I didn't think it was bad. I knew that I had to avoid cops, but everybody did that. Cops never really paid too much attention to a kid anyway. I was at a couple dope spots when they got busted. Everybody would get arrested, and I'd just walk right by. I watched Ice get arrested a few times.

That summer I met Jane in front of CBGBs. She was this gorgeous Puerto Rican chick with a pink and blue leather jacket. There was like a little deviant glow around her. Her face was like a goddess. I liked her a lot, but I was scared to tell her. I told Ice about it, and she made me go talk to her. I just ran up and said, "hi," and then ran away as fast as I could. Ice pushed me back. She actually stood there holding me by my shoulders. But what I didn't know was that Jane had a crush on me too. We started going out right away. She was my girl.

When I was twelve, I started getting into heroin. A few of the people in the squat got me high a few times 'cause they thought it would be funny. Ice beat the shit out of the guy who shot me up and kept screaming at me not to do it. It didn't make sense. I thought that everybody did it, and it was normal. After a few times, I learned how to do it on my own. That was like the greatest thing. It was like, yeah, I'm a grown-up now. I thought I was hot shit. Ice didn't know about it for a while. Sometimes I'd hide her drugs and do them myself. When she found out she flipped.

Pretty soon Jane and I were doing all sorts of drugs, pot, coke, heroin, acid. I used to grab purses in midtown to get the money. I robbed prostitutes and guys trying to buy prostitutes. I'd just grab anything they were holding and run. One time me and Jane were walking down 42nd Street, and this old wino just came out of nowhere and cut her with a broken bottle. I thought he killed her, so I just started pounding on him. I stabbed him with my knife and then broke a couple bottles over his head. The cops rolled up, and I got arrested. They charged me with attempted homicide.

When I went to court, they couldn't find my mom, so they decided to put me in a group home. I had no choice. Within like an hour, these people picked me up and carried me to a van kicking and screaming. We drove to this little farm in Connecticut. When we got out, I just started swinging. I didn't want to be there at all. They had to put me in this rubber time-out room. It took a couple days for me to cool down.

When I got out of the rubber room, they put me to work doing some chores in the kitchen. I went down to the basement for a mop, and I saw a can of gasoline down there. I poured it all over the kitchen. I was just getting ready to light the stove, and this guy came up and tackled me.

They were going to call the cops and put me in a juvenile detention center, but this lady talked them into letting me stay. For two days I had to clean up the gas. When I finished, they let me go into the barn and hang out with the animals. The animals were cool. They were the only thing I didn't try to break or mangle. I didn't want to hang out with other kids. I didn't know how to relate to them, and I was always getting in fights. I even hit one kid with a baseball bat. For the first two weeks, I was in the time-out room every day. All the other times, I was under lock and key, because I was a flight risk.

I didn't trust adults at all. The ones that I met on the streets were always trying to scheme you for sex or something else, even if they were perfectly normal looking—especially if they were perfectly normal looking. The people at the group home freaked me out. They were nice, but they were authoritative. They wanted me to change my clothes and cut my hair, pretty much do everything I didn't want to do. They were really Christian-based people. You had to go to church. You had to say prayers. I didn't like that at all. I'd seen church people before at food kitchens, but you could just blow them off. At the group home they forced you to sit there while they bible-thumped the shit out of you. A week after I tried to burn down the kitchen, they made me kneel down at the altar in front of the priest so that everybody could pray for me. That was really embarrassing. I hated it. Afterwards, the priest talked to me for a while. He was cooler than I thought he'd be, but I didn't want to hear it.

Things didn't get any better as time went on. I knew I wasn't going to get anywhere acting like a maniac, so I started behaving myself to get their trust up. After the third week, they let me go out alone after dinner. It was like seven o'clock, kinda dark. I snuck into the barn where I was hiding my old clothes, then I hauled ass out to the highway and hitchhiked down to Norwalk, Connecticut. I was scared, but I knew I had to do it. From there, I got another ride into Bridgeport. I stayed there for a day and a half on the street. When I panhandled enough cash, I took a train to New York.

From Grand Central I walked back down to the Lower East Side. Everybody was real surprised to see me. I walked up to Ice, and she just jumped up and smothered me with a hug. We were both crying. That was the first day I called her Mom. She cried even more about that. "Mom, I'm home." We were a family. That night, I met up with Jane. She ended up being OK. It wasn't as bad as it looked that night. She had a scar, but it actually kind of enhanced her beauty.

As I got older I became more aware of the squatters movement. The squatters were pretty much like a gang, except there wasn't a designated leader or rights of initiation. If you were a squatter, you were a squatter. We hung out with everybody, the street gangs, the skinheads. It was weird hanging out with the skins, because they believed in one thing, and we believed in another. They had jobs. They were working-class, and we were street scum from the gutters. They pretty much just drank beer, and we did the harder drugs— heroin, coke, PCP. A lot of skins and punks were friends, but we fought too. I guess it was sort of a tense alliance. There were some squatters who became skins and some skins who became squatters. There was a whole squat on 10th Street that was all skinheads.

A lot of things had changed since I first moved to Dos Blockos. A lot of richer people were starting to move into the other buildings, and they didn't like having us around. There was a vigilante group called the Guardian Angels who wanted to get us out of there. They wanted to clean up crime, but after a while it got to be too much. If they saw a kid drinking a beer in the park, they'd beat him up. They beat up a lot of drug dealers, but then some of them were selling drugs themselves. They got away with it, because they'd make citizens arrests on other people. The Guardian Angels turned out to be worse than the street gangs. One day a bunch of them kicked down the door to the squat, and everybody started fighting. A lot of the people I lived with got beat up, even the girls. When it was over, the Guardian Angels took the squat and boarded up the door.

We had been expecting this kind of situation, so we had a plan. There were three people who hid inside the squat, so that we could retake it the next day. All night the Guardian Angels sat guard outside the building. The next night we got all the squatters together and went down there to kick some ass. While we were fighting the Guardian Angels out front, the three people inside ran down and opened the door with sledgehammers. People started running inside and barricading doors. I was on the outside, and it was total chaos. The cops showed up and I got shot in the leg with a beanbag. Then they hit me on the head and dragged me down the street. Ice hit one of the cops, and they let go. We ran all the way back to the park.

By the time we got back to Tompkins, the park was in a riot too. It was madness. Everything was a blur. I remember people laying on the ground, bleeding. People were looting the stores. I saw squatters stomping on cops, and I saw cops stomping squatters. I saw a normal looking guy walking down the street that was getting beat on by everybody. I was running around throwing beer bottles trying to stay away from the cops. It was funny, because I remember that I bought drugs right in the middle of the riot. *(laughs)* My dealer was standing there, and I copped some dope. It was like a little breath from all the madness for a few seconds.

After I got the dope, Ice grabbed me and we ran down Avenue A towards Houston. We took a left on Second and walked back to C. That was the back of the riot. From there, the cops pushed us back in the park. The more we tried to get away from the park, the more we got pushed in. It was like a circle that was squeezing us. Everything started to calm down for a while, but there was still tension. We started walking around in a circle, and every time we made a rotation it got more intense. We were shouting all sorts of things, like "Fuck the police!" and "We're not the enemy!" It was like a mosh pit right before the band starts the music. Then someone hit a drum and everybody went nuts.

I bumped into Jane, and me, her, and Ice busted through the police line and ran over to the West Side. There were no cops over there—none. We sat just off Seventh Avenue and got high. Jane started crying, because one of her friends was still in the park. I wrapped my arms around her, and she said the funniest thing, "You crazy little fucker, why'd you come back home to this?"

After we shot up the dope, we all walked to midtown to stay with some of Ice's friends in a hotel. The cops in midtown were really looking to fuck with us, because we looked like punk rockers. It really saved our ass that we were going into the hotel, because I still had a warrant. We sat in that hotel room for two days. When we got back to the squat, it was trashed. A lot of people were in jail.

Dos Blockos changed after that. It was like a fortress. If the people at the door didn't know you, you couldn't get in. Undercover cops would try to get in there all the time. We'd have to turn our friends away, because they'd be sitting there for hours. Even the people inside couldn't leave, because we'd have to open the door. It was total paranoia for weeks. I was getting the shit kicked out of me by the Guardian Angels on the street.

By that time, Jane and me ended up getting really strung out on heroin. Her dad was always kicking her out of her house, so she was down at the squat a lot. It was getting harder and harder to get money. One night, some guy on Christopher Street was trying to get me to sleep with him. He showed me this fat wad of bills. I had this lead pipe in the sleeve of my jacket, and I smashed him on the head with it. I made off with seven hundred dollars.

I found Ice and Jane in the park, and we bought

a whole lot of heroin. Then we went uptown and got a hotel room. We shot up and then I gave Ice some money to go get some more heroin. Me and Jane already split a bundle, five bags each. It was way more than what we could have done. The most we had ever done before was a bag and a half. We both passed out. When Ice came back, Jane's head was in my lap. Ice looked at her and started screaming. She started shaking her around, but she wasn't moving. We carried her to the corner and called an ambulance. Ice had to drag me away so the police wouldn't find us. I sat there crying in the hotel room for the whole night.

I'm the one who fixed the shots. I'm the one who handed her the shot. I told her everything was going to be all right, but it wasn't. That was my first love. A month before that, I asked her to marry me on St. Marks. She said yeah.

The next day I was in the park, and Jane's dad showed up looking for the guy who sold her the drugs. He knew I was her boyfriend, and he grabbed me and slammed me against the fence. I told him I didn't know what happened. I said we got into an argument and she left with some guy. It was a total lie. I gave him the description of this guy who didn't exist. To this day, if he found out, he'd probably kill me. He's got every right. We both broke out in tears. When I went to Jane's funeral, her dad gave me back the ring that I gave her. I took my ring off and put it on her finger.

Right after that, Ice tested positive for HIV. She went off the deep end. She started doing more dope and a lot of coke. Every night she kept telling me to quit doing this shit. Then one night, she went out and hit a two bundle shot and killed herself.

I pretty much lost it after that—just walking around crying, beating up cars, getting high, fighting.

I wanted to die too. I was out of control. I started to have problems with the people in the squat. They knew that Ice was my mom, so at first they gave me some slack, but I didn't care. Eventually, I got kicked out.

I stayed in the park and sold heroin. Once in a while, I'd get a hotel room. I was doing a lot of drugs and pretty much trying to do the same thing Ice was—kill myself. Then one day I met a bunch of travelers who came in from Hollywood. I had always heard how great the punk scene was out there, and they really hyped it up. It was starting to get kind of chilly, so I started hitchhiking west. I was pretty miserable from kicking on the road.

Hollywood was like heaven. There were hundreds of punk rockers everywhere. It was beautiful. The people were a lot more laid back. At first, I got into a couple fights because I had that New York attitude, but once I realized that I didn't have to be like that, everything was great. I made a lot of friends really quick and ended up staying in a squat about five minutes into Hollywood. The people there said my name Unwanted was too depressing, and they changed it to Bolt, because I had metal bolts sewed into my jacket.

Seeing Ice and Jane die from heroin made me lay off the dope for a while. Instead I started doing a lot of speed. I stayed out on the streets for weeks at a time. I didn't have to eat. I didn't have to sleep. I didn't have to do anything. At first I was still pretty depressed, but after a year things were starting to get better. I met a new girlfriend, we had sex maybe twice. I was still kind of weird about that, because the only girl I really wanted was Jane. This girl kind of reminded me of Jane a little bit, and that helped me get over everything.

There was a lot of tension in Hollywood right

before the Rodney King riots. We all knew the riot was going to happen, but nobody said anything. Everybody was walking around with that hungry wolf look in their eyes, looking for victims. It started downtown first, and all the cops went down there. There was no cops in Hollywood at all. We were out on the sidewalk drinking, and we were all thinking about going downtown. Then we heard these people shouting farther down on Hollywood Boulevard. It just swept right past us. People were smashing things and grabbing stuff out of stores. There was one guy running by with a TV. He tripped and smashed the TV on the sidewalk. Two minutes later, he came running by with a new TV. Everybody was cheering.

At first I just watched, but when somebody threw a brick at one of the head shops, I went in and grabbed some clothes. I didn't do a lot of looting, because I got started kind of late, and I was worried about my own ass. The cops were sectioning areas off and pushing people out. Gradually they'd let you back in, but you couldn't walk in a group bigger than three people.

For months after the Rodney King riots, the cops really started cracking down on us. It was sort of like revenge. A lot of the squatters started leaving LA. After a few months, there were only about twenty kids left. I drove up to San Francisco with a bunch of people in the back of my friend Black Cat's truck. I slept in Golden Gate Park. Nothing really eventful happened, just a lot of drugs. I was still doing speed, and I started doing heroin again. I hung out with a lot of different people, but nobody ever stuck around for long.

Frisco got boring after a year, so I hopped a train up to Seattle. Six of us got in a boxcar with a bunch of beer and dope. It was beautiful. I've never seen trees that big before. My friends were like, "What are you, a hippie?"

Seattle was boring. I stayed on the sidewalks for a while, and then I moved into a squat. I sold dope for a while, but I had to stop when the cops kicked everybody out of the squat. In '93, I hopped a train back to Frisco.

I stayed in Golden Gate Park for another six months selling speed. That was a lot different than selling dope. When you sell dope, people are calm, you might have to listen to some real sad stories from dope-sick junkies with no money, but with speed these people won't leave you alone. They're all tweaked out and spun all crazy out of their minds.

In '94 I left Frisco and went back down to LA. Hollywood changed drastically since I'd left. There were hardly any punks there at all. I stayed there for about six months, then I had to leave because the cops were fucking with me so much.

It was during the whole grunge thing, so I decided to go back to Seattle. Kurt Cobain was having his heyday, and that was the place to be. It was cool at first, but after a while I kind of got sick of it. The grunge thing was basically just a bunch of rich kids slumming it. When Kurt blew his brains out, I thought that was the funniest thing in the world.

At the end of '95 I headed back to Frisco. I met some people who made LSD, and we decided to take a bunch of sheets out to Tucson to make some cash. That's where I got my facial tats. I was walking through a street fair on Fourth Avenue and I bumped into this guy who was looking for acid. I was selling tabs for five bucks a hit for anything under ten. He was looking to get ten hits, but he didn't have any money. Then he told me he was a tattoo artist. I just threw it out in the air. I said, "I'll give you a sheet if you do my forehead and my face right now." He said OK. I looked through the book, and checked out some pictures. I couldn't get exactly what I wanted, but it was pretty close. When he was done, I got up from the chair and ran over to this punk rock show with blood running down my face. I had so much adrenaline that I didn't even bother putting Vaseline on it. When I got into the show, everybody flipped out. Anything on your face is taboo. It's such a shock. I love it.

Things were going good in Arizona, but I missed New York and wanted to go back. I got a ride with some people into Denver, and I stayed there for two days in a squat. On the second day the cops busted in and caught me drinking a half-gallon of whiskey. They arrested me because I was from New York, and I was the oldest. They charged me with criminal trespassing, vandalism, public nuisance and disturbing the peace. It was fucked up, because I didn't even have any drugs on me. I wasn't hurting anybody. We went to trial, and they ended up giving me six months in the state lock-up.

Being in jail sucks. The worst day that I've had on the street is better than the best day in prison. It's a constant struggle. You can't back down from anybody. People were kind of scared of my facial tats, but I still had to earn my respect. One time I was in the same cell as a child molester. It looked bad on me to be living with him, so I beat him up. The second guy was this black kid who tried to take my canteen. Then, there was this one guy bragging about how he beat up his seven-year-old kid. I was living with a bunch of Nazis, so to gain more respect, I jumped up and beat him up.

When I got out of jail, they decided to place me in a halfway house in Denver for another six months. I was there for like two days, and then I took off for San

Francisco. I ended up getting real strung out, and I passed out on the beach. The cops fingerprinted me, and they found out about my warrants.

Two US marshals flew me back to Denver. I had to wear these knee-brace things so that I could walk but couldn't run. They had shackles all over me. We sat with the regular people in the coach section. They were all tripped out about it. It was actually kind of fun. The marshals were cool, they let me smoke a cigarette once we landed. When we got back to the court-house, they wanted to give me six years. My public defender got it dropped down to three.

Once I finished my time in Denver, they let me out on parole. I didn't know anybody in Colorado, so I headed back to New York. It was '97. I hadn't been home in like ten years. Right outside of Philly I was in this pizza shop, and this cop just came up out of nowhere and asked me for ID. They sent me back to prison in Denver for parole violation. I did four months, then I went back to Tucson for three months. I got arrested when I was really drunk, and I got sent back. This time they wouldn't give me parole, so I had to finish my entire sentence in prison. I just got out a year and a half ago. Now I've got no parole, no probation, nothing. I'm rather enjoying that.

It was getting near wintertime, so I decided to head back to San Francisco. I met some squatters, and we moved into a place on Second and Mission. It was Anton LaVey's house, the founder of the original Church of Satan. It's where they wrote *The Satanic Bible*, *The Satanic Witch*, *Devil's Notebook*, *Satan Speaks*. When Anton LaVey died, Blanch Burton stole all the money, and she sold the house and split. By the time we got there, it was in pretty rough shape, and they were getting ready to tear it down.

It was freaky. There were trap doors and hidden passageways everywhere. I could get from the third floor to the basement without walking through a room or doorway. You could walk right up behind somebody, grab their hat, and disappear. We found the first door by accident. It was like a movie.

I still had the prison mentality, so I didn't talk to hardly anybody. I did a lot of scams to get money for dope like robbing people or stealing bikes. Once I robbed this guy for two thousand seven hundred dollars. When that money ran out, I started cutting down on the dope. I went from a three-gram-a-day black-tar heroin habit to a half gram a day. I was trying to kick, because I wanted to get off the streets and retire. That's when I met Stephanie.

Bolt and Stephanie

Having recorded Bolt and Stephanie's interviews up to the point where they met, I decide to complete their stories together. On a brisk night in early November I find them sitting at the picnic tables in East River Park surrounded by at least a dozen other regulars from Crusty Lane. The sweet smell of barbecue permeates the autumn air, and. Bolt greets me eagerly and offers me a pork chop.

A bunch of people got their food stamps today. Wanna eat some pigs?

Groups of wanderers filter in and out. Bread is broken, and bottles are passed. After the barbecue dies down, Bolt suggests that we start a campfire in one of the barbecue grills. Five or six people break off into groups to scour the park for fallen branches. I leave my briefcase at the table and join the hunt. It seems ironic to be fulfilling such a primal function sandwiched between the belittling monstrosity of the Williamsburg Bridge and the drab glow of the projects on Avenue D. Bolt takes charge of constructing the fire.

If I could rule the world, this whole fucking thing would be covered in flames. Those who didn't like it, well they'd get the firing squad—and their family has to pay for bullets. *Bolt withdraws a burning stick from the fire and whirls it around his head.* The Jedi craves a beer. Must use The Force. *Bolt's friend Chaos hands him a bottle of Colt 45.* See, it works. But a Jedi warrior seeks action and adventure. He seeks not the things that I'm looking for. I'm going to the Dark Side. Fuck it.

Chaos: You know what's funny? In every comic, the bad guy looks like a punk rocker.

Bolt: So I guess we're all supermodels.

Chaos: Even at the end of GI Joe, who's smashing the windows? Punk rockers. *Bolt smashes a bottle in the fire. Chaos continues in a mocking straightforward tone.* You shouldn't do that. Glass is a commodity, and as an American, we value our commodities. GI Joe says, Don't do blow. Fuck that shit. Cobra!

Bolt: But the worst thing is the kids who wanna be punks. You know what's so funny? I saw a fucking kid on St. Marks all punked out wearing a Manny Basker patch, and I'm all like hey that's some fucking cool tags, and I started singing one of their songs. He looked at me like I didn't know what the fuck was up. I was like, you don't even know anything about what you're wearing. You fucking moron. Here, give me your mohawk, SNIP!

The campfire circle breaks when we hear the snarling yelps of two dogs attacking each other down by the river. A quarrel develops between the two owners. Bolt and Stephanie watch for a few moments and then step to the side.

Bolt: Hey babe, the middle packet of my bag, can you get my gear? Oh shit, I forgot to get water. Hey Chaos, got any water?

Chaos: Sorry, I don't drink.

At first the references to "gear" and the sudden urgency for water leave me puzzled. When I look back over at the picnic table, I see several people have discreetly engaged in the intricate process of shooting up. Bolt and Stephanie cook up their heroin with vodka, but I hear this anonymous conversational fragment:

"Can I use some of your water?"

"It's dirty. I got Hep B and C really bad."

After all of the needles have been rinsed and stowed away, I follow Bolt and Stephanie south along the FDR to the decaying ruins of the East River Park bandshell. We enter though a portion of the fence that has been removed with wire cutters.

I gaze out at the decaying grandstands that once held thousands of spectators. It seems a shame that such a valuable community resource could go to waste.* Slowly we traipse through the surrealist landscape into the interior of the rotting structure. Stephanie and I climb a ladder up to the couple's private sleeping area in the rafters. Bolt follows behind with the squealing Anubis in his arms.

Steph: What the fuck? It stinks like piss up here.

Bolt: Anubis pissed on the floor this morning, stu-

---

*The old bandshell has since been demolished and new construction is underway.

pid asshole.

Bolt and Stephanie settle into the corner. They speak in dreary monotones as they stare through the holes in the roof at the star-sprinkled sky.

Bolt: I just got kicked out of the Ramada Inn the night I met Stephanie. I came out of this store, and I saw my friend Art walking down the street with her. You were with Jimmy too, right, babe?

Steph: Yeah, it was me, Art, Julio, Jimmy and Tweaker Josh.

Bolt: Anyway, Art told me that they were going to go hang out at this punk show, and I went with them. We were sitting in the alley, and Steph went and bought some beers. I was going to throw in a dollar, but she said it was OK. She had a job. I thought wow, this girl's really cool, she's really cute too. I had the hots for her immediately. *Stephanie laughs.*
At first Stephanie's friend Jimmy didn't like me, because I stole one of his friend's girlfriends. This guy was sending all these nasty emails saying I was a Nazi, but once Jimmy got to know me, he knew it wasn't true. His friend was just jealous because I was fucking his girl better than he was.

Steph (softly): Oh, Christ.

Bolt: It's true! She even told him that. *Stephanie rolls her eyes mockingly.*
I talked to Stephanie for a while that night. When I told her about the Church of Satan, she was really excited to go see it. She wrote down where she worked

and said that if I stopped by the next day she'd give me a free meal. I liked her immediately. *(laughs)*

Steph: Bolt kept hitting on me in the alley. He was like, "Hey you should come to the Church of Satan and spend the night—you can only get the full effect if you stay the night—with me."

Bolt: I wasn't hitting on you! God!

Steph: I was just like, oh yeah, another guy hitting on me. I thought he was cute, but I thought I'd never see him again.

Bolt: That night, construction workers came and welded up the door to the Church. I wanted to go see Stephanie the next day—I had the hots for her—but it took us until six at night to get the door open. By the time I got downtown it was like eight.

Steph: When Bolt didn't show up, I wasn't surprised. I didn't really care, because there were a couple other dudes who I was watching. Then, a couple days later, me and my friend Jimmy drove downtown, and we saw Bolt walking down the street. Jimmy wanted to go to the Church of Satan pretty bad, so I told him to run after him. I was scared, because I thought that Jimmy was going to tell Bolt that I liked him. That would have been embarrassing.

Bolt hung out with us all day. We went to the Anarchist Book Fair, and that night there was a keg party on the beach. I blew off my curfew at Grer House and decided to head up to the Church of Satan with Bolt. He was a cute guy, so I said fuck it.

When I went up to the door, it felt like something

was staring at me, like someone was going to jump out and stab me in the back. But once you got into the house it was like this calm washed over you. It was awesome. There were demons painted all over the walls and pentagrams on the floors. In the kitchen there was this big mural of Satan destroying a city.

Bolt: That night I talked to Stephanie for like four hours. We had a lot of friends in common from Hollywood and Frisco. The cool thing about being a traveling kid is that everybody knows everybody. I really wanted to hit on Stephanie, but I was pretty drunk, and I passed out. That morning, we got kicked out of the squat by construction workers again. We hung out all day, but that night they welded the door shut again. I didn't have anywhere to go, so Stephanie snuck me into Grer House.

Steph: It was kind of a hassle getting him in. I had to wait till it was really late, then I had to sneak him up the back staircase. That night, the staff kept checking my room, and I had to hide Bolt in the shower. I think they knew something was up. Maybe my roommate snitched me out, which was kind of fucked up, because her boyfriend was up there all the time.

Bolt: I think my facial tats freaked her out.

Between the staff people coming in, Steph and I made out. We didn't have sex, but it was really cool. We both copped a feel on each other. It was cool, because we didn't have sex right away. I don't want a one-night stand. I'm a one-woman kind of guy, but I tried to have sex with her just to see. She kept saying no. That made me like her so much more.

In the morning the counselor came in and asked

Stephanie why her bed was moved. I was lying there with this huge pile of blankets on top of me. The counselor told me to come out, but I wouldn't move. It was actually kind of stupid, because my feet were sticking out. Then she said they were gonna call the cops if I didn't get up. Everybody was screaming. They didn't even let me get my clothes. I had to go out on the street in a T-shirt and my underwear.

Steph: I was trying to get all my stuff together, because they pretty much told me that I had to leave too. I was like whoa, because I had all those court issues. I told Bolt to go outside and wait on the corner while I packed. Fifteen minutes later, I went outside and he was nowhere around. I was like great, that fucking sucks. I thought he went downtown to cop, and I wasn't ever going to see him again. That asshole, that piece of shit—and I got kicked out of my house for that motherfucker. I was FUCKED. I hadn't been squatting for a year, and I didn't know where to go.

Bolt: I was at the store! I spanged up like a dollar and I got a soda. That's why she missed me! After like an hour, I saw her walking down the street. I asked her if she wanted to stay with me, and she said yeah. We camped out that night, and it was kind of chilly. The next night, I was like fuck it. Tonight we're going back to the Church. We stayed up all night getting drunk and talking, then we passed out. That was another time we didn't have sex. We didn't have sex for like what? Almost two weeks?

I already knew that I loved her, but I didn't want to say it, cause I didn't want to scare her away. The feelings were there. I loved the shit out of her like the fourth day we were together. I told all my friends, and they thought I was crazy. They told me I was just pussy whipped, but we hadn't fucked yet. We were just always holding hands and getting mushy and giggly. It was the first time I was happy in about *(whistles)* eight years. We used to talk all night long.

What type of stuff did you talk about?

Steph: We were pretty much into the same stuff, all the same music. We pretty much did all the same shit. The day after I got kicked out of Grer House, I started shooting dope again.

Bolt: I was really dope sick, and I asked Stephanie for twenty bucks. She copped it with me. At first, I didn't want to give her any, but she was like, "Fuck it. Give me a rinse." So I gave her a really fat rinse. The next day, I copped again, and I gave her another rinse. I was like tomorrow you can't do it, because it's the third day. But I gave her a rinse on the third day. The fourth day she said, "Fuck it, let's go split a half." We started shooting dope on a regular basis, about two grams a day for the both of us.

Steph: I was really worried about what was going to happen with my probation officer after I got kicked out of Grer House. I just told her that I was living with a friend, and she let me slide. I only had one month left anyway. Everything was working out great. I was getting fake piss all the time, so I didn't test any dirties. I was going to NA meetings and getting papers signed. I still had my job at the restaurant.

With two weeks left I went to see my probation officer. She pulled some shit out of nowhere. She said I wasn't ready, and that they were going to keep me on probation for another three months. WHAT THE FUCK? I freaked out. I was like fuck you and left. I never reported since.

Bolt: By then we cracked open another squat and started staying in there. It was right on 12th and Folson, right across the street from where Stephanie worked. In the morning she used to leave twenty bucks on the table, and when I woke up, which was usually about two o'clock, I'd go cop and then get Stephanie at work. Then we'd shoot up together.

It was cool. Me and her did something different every day. I was like, this rocks. I found a girl I could talk to about my dreams. Like I really want to go to New Zealand, because everybody down there has facial tats, and it's accepted. Stephanie knew this guy from New Zealand, and she told me stories about it. We just connected. We never argued. Except one day she gave me the twenty dollars and I shot up all the dope myself. I tried to make the money back before her work was over, but I couldn't. I lied to her. I fucked up bad, and I thought that she was gonna hate me. But I walked back to her work anyway, because I had to.

Steph: No you didn't.

Bolt: No no. That was a different time when I went and copped that crack for that other dude on Market. But that first time, Steph just kinda forgave me, cause she said she knew I was gonna do it anyway.

Steph: That's right. The next day, I gave him some money and told him to get me some dope. He doesn't show up. I was laying on the back couch at work, sick as fuck. I go down to 6th and Market, and I see him, right? He just walks right by me with some guy. I was like, "HEY! What the fuck!" He told me that he was going to buy some crack for this dude. Now, he knew that I hated crack. I was like fuck you! I pretty much thought that it was over. He already fucked me over twice, and that was enough.

Bolt: But I wasn't smoking the crack! I was just trying to swing a deal for this kid to make some cash. I ran after her and explained it. For like four hours I had to convince her that I wasn't smoking crack. I guess I kinda fucked up, because I didn't show up at her work. I just wanted to go and make some money so that I could have something to show her.

After two months, Steph started getting real paranoid about her probation officer, and she needed to get the fuck out of there. I started talking to her about going to New York. I was ready to go home. I had an awesome girl, and things couldn't have been better. It was like I had a family. I also had this little kid that I adopted named Shwilly. He came to me one night for protection after he got jumped.

Steph: I was trying to save up enough money to buy a van, but I didn't have enough, so I bought three Greyhound tickets for me, Shwilly, and Bolt.

Bolt: Normally I would have hitchhiked, but we didn't want to take a chance with Steph on probation. We were doing dope the whole Greyhound ride, and I was telling her about the Lower East Side and how great it was. I hadn't been home in forever.

Steph: The day before we got to New York, we were in Chicago trying to cop in the ghetto. It was sketchy.

These black people jacked us up against the wall to see if we had guns. They really ripped us off cause we only got two bags for forty bucks. After we copped, we were walking all over the place with these squatter kids. They had this game where they'd run up behind each other and kick each other's foot. It was like Charlie Brown football. Bolt went to go kick Shwilly, and he ended up kicking me right on my leg. AHHHHHHHH!!! My leg hurt so bad I could hardly walk.

Bolt: Sorry, baby.

Steph: We missed the bus, so we had to spend two more days in Chicago before we could get another one. We couldn't score dope anywhere. We were dope sick as shit. When we got into New York, we had to walk all the way from Port Authority to the Lower East Side. The whole way, Bolt was telling me all these horror stories. I was scared to even ask anyone for a cigarette. We went into Tompkins Square, and nothing was like the way Bolt said it was. He really didn't know anybody other than this big fat guy, Frenchy the Scamp.[*]

Bolt: I was really psyched to see Frenchy. I heard this rumor that he was dead and there he was. I jumped up and gave him a big hug. I introduced him to Stephanie, and he started fucking with her, like tickling her, just being Frenchy. Steph was kind of freaked out, but he does that to all my girlfriends. He was like, "That's right. I do it to all his girlfriends. Why? Because I'm Frenchy the Scamp. That's why."

---

[*]I conducted a brief interview with Frenchy in early July. It was difficult to establish rapport, and I was unable to elicit a coherent story. Later that day I taped over his interview. Frenchy died of a heroin overdose in September.

Steph: After that, we went to go cop dope on Avenue D and walked down to East River Park to shoot up. Bolt bumped into a few more people he knew. It was all right, but we were worried about how we were going to make money.

Then like out of nowhere, this guy comes down and asks us if we wanted a job holding up these huge signs in midtown. We were like yeah. We got in a van, and he drove us to 42nd Street. We just had to stand there in front of the store. It paid fifty bucks a day. We used to have light-saber fights with the signs. *(laughs)*

Bolt: Every day when the van dropped us off from work, we'd get a bag and get high. We were buying a bundle a day. It was pretty cool hanging out with the squatter kids. In July we adopted our dog Anubis* from somebody who was heading out west.

Anubis isn't our dog, he's our son, our little boy. He's got his own jacket, with his own money. He's got a raincoat, a sweatshirt. He's got more gear than me and Steph. We love the shit out of this dog.

One night we were down here at East River Park, and the moon was sitting out over Brooklyn, and it was just gigantic. We saw two pennies sitting there heads up on the walkway, and we each threw one into the river and made a wish. Stephanie asked me what my wish was, and I got down on my knees and asked her to marry me. She said yes. I jumped up and gave her a kiss. I kept asking her like fifty times over and over again. It wasn't like a real ceremony, we just agreed that we wanted to be together.

Steph: It's like a squat marriage. Like, do you take

---

*Anubis is the Egyptian god of the underworld.

this filthy-ass whore to be your awfully decrepit bitch for the rest of your rotten squattin' life till the grave? Yes, I take this fucking bitch to be my whore.

Bolt: Do you take this asshole to be your man, to bitch at, and put up with his sorry-ass shit for the rest of your miserable life?

In the beginning of August the guy with the van stopped coming by to pick us up. We didn't have any money, so we had to start kicking dope. For two days it hurt really bad. We wanted to get some more dope, but all we had was change from panhandling. Dealers won't take change, so I asked this lady if she had a dollar bill for four quarters. She just snorted and looked the other way. I was like, "Well fuck you then, bitch. You can take that dollar, roll it up real tight, and shove it in your ass!" This big jock looking guy was sitting on the same stoop. I think it was her boyfriend. He was all getting up in my face, so I pulled out a can of mace and said, "Look, I don't feel like fighting right now." Then he pulled out a gun.

Stephanie started screaming, "Oh my god don't shoot him!" I ran across St. Marks, and three cops just tackled me from out of nowhere. Anubis came running over and got underneath a cop. He bit me on the jaw, and then bit down on my shoulder. I think that he was trying to pull me away from there. I was bleeding so much that I passed out right in the street.

Steph: The cops were stomping all over him.

Bolt: They took me to Central Booking, and I got charged with assault and possession of heroin. I stayed downtown for three days, kicking cold turkey. Then I went to Riker's for twenty-one days and got methadone. I was flipping out. I didn't care about myself, but I was worried about Steph. She was in New York and she hardly knew anybody. I thought maybe she'd go back to San Francisco.

They were talking about giving me eight years, but when I went to court they had to drop the charges, because the cops lied. All the names on the witness list were fictitious. When I left the courthouse, I ran as fast as I could to Tompkins Square. Stephanie was just sitting there on a bench. Anubis started growling as soon as I came up. She picked her head up and looked at me like "Who the fuck are you?" Right there, my heart broke. I was getting ready to walk away and curl up and cry. But then her face changed, and I saw that sparkle in her eye. It was like WHAM, and she just tackled me with a big hug.

Steph: It really sucked when Bolt got arrested. We were staying here in the bandshell, and one night it got raided. Shwilly took off, and it was just me and Anubis. A few nights after that this guy stole all this jewelry, and he ended up getting real pissed off and throwing it everywhere. I picked it up and started selling it on the street to get money for dope.

Since Bolt got back we've had some good times, but it's been kind of rocky too. We were here when the towers went down, and we saw the second plane hit. I had just started working at this place downtown called Sexy Chat Dot Com, and the satellite communications went down, so I lost my job. Since then we've just been hanging out down here. These days, we're doing about four bags a day each. We'll do one in the morning, one in the afternoon, and a two-bag shot at night.

It's starting to get pretty cold at night, so we're thinking of hopping a train down to New Orleans.

We're also really scared about the anthrax. I don't know how that's going to work out, because since this terrorist thing happened, it's going to be really tough security on the trains. We'll probably just hitchhike.

Bolt: For future, don't fuck with Osama bin Laden.

Steph: Fuck that jackass piece of shit.

Bolt: We've been panhandling real hard trying to get enough money for the trip. Every now and then, some stupid fifteen-year-old ravers will walk up to us and ask us to buy X. We just take the money. Last night this kid gave me a hundred dollars. There's a lot of suckers. Plus, I'm doing these kids a favor. Ecstasy is a really fucked up drug. They should call it misery.

I'm looking to retire when we get down to New Orleans. Just move into a place and get fat and watch TV—and she's gonna work. *(laughs)* I'm gonna be the housewife.

Me, Stephanie, and Anubis are a family. Even though we argue a lot—because we're all strung out. I see us being together for...

Steph: A very long time.

Bolt and Stephanie find a ride south two days later.

James Carter
Yonkers, New York 1967

I first meet James on a bright morning in July. Dressed in a clean button-down shirt and sipping from a bottle of iced tea, he looks no different from any other standard-issue East Villager. When he approaches and asks about my tape recorder, I find out that he is currently looking for a job and trying to pull himself off the street. James is very eager to tell me his story, and he enunciates his responses with cathartic vigor.

My father ran his own tailor shop uptown on 141st and St. Nicholas. In 1971 he bought a house for thirty thousand dollars in South Yonkers. My two sisters and me were the only kids, because my brother was twenty years older and going to college. My father sent all of his kids to college except for me.

Back in the seventies, it was a privilege for me to be black and live in a middle-class neighborhood. We were on the more upscale side of the tracks, newer houses with newer money. They used take us black kids on busses to other schools in North Yonkers so that they could have a ten percent black student pop ulation. That was a good experience, because I learned about rock and roll from the middle class white kids. One of my best friends had a punk group called Fat Head Suburbia. He wanted to take me to CBGBs, but I was scared. We traded tapes, and I was into the culture, but as a black kid, I didn't have the balls to dress that way. My school and my neighborhood were different worlds. Like, I couldn't wear a rock and roll T-shirt on my block. People would call me a sellout.

My father was real big on education. He wanted me to be better off than he was. Like if you see his handwriting you would think it was a school kid's, but he knew math, and that's what saved him. My brother took from that and got real good at calculus. Today he's a nuclear engineer. My sister's a paralegal. If it weren't for my addiction, I'm sure that I'd be right up there with them.

The first time I smoked crack was in 1985. I was seventeen. Everything was going good in life. I had a job working at Shop Rite. I even had a car. One day my friend's older brother asked me for a ride to the city. We drove down into Washington Heights and bought some crack. A vial cost twenty dollars then and we shared it. I was just curious and I wanted to try it.

Then crack started moving to the Bronx, where it was closer to Yonkers. I started going down more often. One day I said let me smoke a whole rock instead of breaking it up. That was a big rush it was so intense that I fell in love with it. It was better than sex. It took the place of girls. It took the place of hanging out at the skating rink, playing video games. My childhood was OVER as I had known it.

I would sleep, smoke, and stare into space, basically enjoy the wave. *(laughs)* When I came down, I would fiend. I sold my stereo, and then one day I stole my father's wallet with like two hundred dollars in it. I lied and said I used it for this girl's abortion. That night I went down to the city and bought five vials. When I got back they ended up being stale breadcrumbs. The same night I went back with another fifty dollars and scored. When I got back, I started smoking it in my parents' bathroom. My mother started banging on the door, and I just froze. I finished smoking the rocks, and my dad busted in on me. He told me that I needed to stop or I was gonna die.

A few days later, I was creeping on my stomach to

steal my father's wallet a second time. The light came on and he jumped up. MOTHER FUCKER!!! BOWWWW!!! He shot at me with a gun. It was just a scare tactic, but it really shook me up. I ran from the house and came back hours later begging him. He talked to me and told me that I had to leave. He basically forced me to join the Army.

Basic training was the roughest experience of my life. You walked around like robots. Everything in that barrack had to be spit polished. They didn't even let you smoke cigarettes. When I finished basic training and went to my permanent duty assignment, I was shocked. The barracks were like a fraternity house, full of beer bongs and kegs. People were out in the back barbecuing. I loved it. I met different kinds of kids from all over the country and saw a lot of new things. Like I was used to eating grits with butter and salt, but I saw people putting sugar on it. It was a totally different world. I thought that all the Southern white folks would try to kill all the black folks, but it wasn't like that. We were like brothers. If we had to fight, it would be black and white together for our company, I Company 227 3rd Armor Division. That was what you represented.

After a few months our unit got sent to a base near Frankfurt, Germany. My MOS, or job, was a diesel truck mechanic. I worked on jeeps all the way up to ten-ton trucks. I was proud of it, because I was good. It was like a puzzle. I had a good work ethic, and the sergeants liked me. They could count on James. James would be there when he was told to be and get the job done.

I still maintained my addiction through the Army. There wasn't any crack, but there was alcohol. That was promoted to be used as a social thing. The sergeant always said, "I don't trust a man who doesn't drink." It was pretty much pushed down your throat. I started drinking pretty hard, and I'd get into fights. That's how I got my fake tooth. I was a blackout drinker, and I wouldn't remember what happened. One time a German girl stabbed me in the leg *(pulls up pants to show a scar)*. Word about this got back to my superior officers, and they gave me an R15, non-judicial punishment. They could have kicked me out, but I was valuable to them as a soldier. Instead they made me go to treatment. I had to take a pill called Antabuse. If you tried to drink when you were on Antabuse, you'd get violently sick.

One night, I was hanging out with some girls at a club called the Funkadelic in Frankfurt—cool clothes, girls—the place to be. We met some local girls, and they said lets go get high. They hooked us up with some hashish and heroin. Heroin made me DRUNK! It was like an alcohol high without the hangover. See I didn't do enough to get the dope sickness, so there weren't any negative consequences. I still had my faculties, so I wasn't fighting or scaring away pretty girls. I fell in love with it. That's been haunting me for ten years.

Pretty soon my habit got to the point where I was going down to Frankfurt every day. When I got high, I would do weird stuff. Once, I was watching that movie *Sid and Nancy* about the Sex Pistols, and I started poking at my arms with a pin, because that's what Sid Vicious was doing in the movie. It got to the point where I either had to quit heroin, or the officers would find out. Drugs are taboo in the army. Plus, they had snitches. You could be real close with somebody, and they'd rat you out for a court martial in a second.

I decided to go cold turkey on my own. I was real

sick for a few days, but I did it. After that I started being a better soldier. My uniform looked sharp, and they promoted me to a specialist. I was looking into getting certified as an X ray technician.

Things were going good. I met this fraulein Gretchen who wanted to domesticate me. I lived with her, and we played house. She would cook for me just like a wife. Eventually, she talked me into leaving the army so that we could live together as civilians. I had two jobs, and I was going to school. She was working too, and we both had cars. Then Gretchen ended up pregnant. It wasn't that bad of a situation. See in Germany people take you for who you are. There's no real racists.

Things were looking good, but then I found out how to get cocaine. I was at a bar drinking a couple beers, and the next thing you know, I was freebasing. I spent my savings up, and I stole from Gretchen. Then I cheated on her and she found out. I had told her before that if I ever start using drugs to get away from me, because I turn into a monster. That's what she did. Her family gave me a five hundred dollar plane ticket and sent me back to New York.

I went to see my mother in Yonkers. That lasted about a minute, because she knew what I had been up to. She said she didn't want to see her baby son kill himself, and she kicked me outta the house. It was like I was on a suicide mission. I lost my girlfriend. I lost my lifestyle—being respected—being a man. I also had a son who I was never going to see.

I ended up drifting through the Bronx, spending some nights on the street and bouncing in and out of shelters. It was hell. I was dirty, hungry, chasing drugs—always going to scary neighborhoods to cop. The other homeless people at that time were like mentally ill bums. I was walking around with an army C bag digging in dumpsters for cans. Finally, I went to the Veterans Domiciliary in St. Albans, Queens.

That program worked because I had peers with a similar military background. These guys were Vietnam Vets, so they knew the meaning of comradeship. Cigarettes, coffee, and food took the place of beer, cocaine, and heroin. They sent me to school to become a nurse's aide. When I started working with AIDS patients at Bellevue, that really shocked me and made me think about how precious life is.

After fifteen months I graduated the program and got my own apartment in Long Island City. I was doing volunteer work and getting social service checks. Things were starting to fall back into place, and people were happy for me. I was going back over to my mother's house for dinner in my nurse uniform, and she would show me off to her girlfriends. One thing that I really enjoyed was going out at night down to the AA meetings on St. Marks.

Then the same shit always happens—a girl fucked it up. Just like Adam and Eve with the apple, but instead of the apple, it's dope. I was in St. Marks Meeting House one night, and I met this Greek woman from Astoria named Eliana. She floored me. She dressed like Jackie O—nice hat and nice clothes. One night, she walked into the meeting high as a kite. That got me thinking about the good old days when I used to sniff dope. Next thing you know I'm in Tompkins Square.

This place was out of control. I saw the crusty punks, the gutter punks, and that really turned me on. It reminded me of high school. I started hanging out with that crew, and they hooked me up with heroin and fifty-cent beers. It was kind of scary for me, because back in '95, this was still the ghetto, almost all Hispanic. I didn't fit in, because I'd wear an Izod shirt and tight jeans with Oxford shoes.

I ended up bringing girls back to my place in Queens, they'd eat my food up, and steal my change. I was basically using them for sex. One time I brought a dealer back to Queens and he just trashed my place. When the VA caught on, they kicked me out of the extended care program.

I ended up going into another program in Albany, but I just didn't have the desire, and I ended up back out on the street. The drugs up in Albany cost twice as much as here. I went to a church up there, and they gave me a ticket back to New York. I ended up living in Tompkins and sleeping on 9th Street.

As the years slipped by, people started dying. One friend went out a third story window in St. Marks Hotel. I know another girl who hung herself in Riker's Island. There were ODs left and right. People were getting AIDS. I saw people just picking up needles off the ground. They were dropping like flies. If all the ghosts came back to Tompkins, the place would be so packed you couldn't even walk.

I used to panhandle for money, then I'd hit Kmart and start boosting stuff. I'd go in with a flannel shirt and start stuffing disposable cameras. Then I'd walk out, sell the shit, and get maybe twenty bucks if I was lucky. I always tried to keep a respectable appearance, because you can't go into a store looking like a piece of shit, or security will be on you. All the money went to drugs. I probably wouldn't have eaten if it wasn't for Trinity Church and the Salvation Army trucks. When the wintertime came, I'd go into shelters. I went four years like that.

When I first came to the park it was about partying and having a good time. I'd sit at this place called Downtown Beirut and drink eight-dollar pitchers. You could sniff your dope in the bathroom and then relax with your friends. Those were the good old days. But once I got caught in the grips of my addiction, there was no more of that, no friends, no girls, just the next score, trying to stay one step ahead of the TNT street crime unit.

Once Giuliani came in, I started getting busted for possession. I even got arrested for a B felony for just being there at a drug deal. I went to Riker's for the first time at thirty. I felt like a fool, because I didn't know how to use the phone. I was lucky that my court case was dismissed, but when I got out I was stuck in the same shit—hanging out in the park.

An energetic man strolls down the walkway shouting, "White van, sandwiches, juice and cookies!"

Did you hear about the guy who fed the people in the park a dead girl? He used to cut himself and say he was Jesus Christ. He killed his girlfriend, chopped her up and made a stew out of it, then he served it to the people in this park. They found out because there was a finger in it. He kept the bones in a locker in Port Authority. They put him in a psyche ward instead of jail. That's some wild shit.

Then two years ago, these three gutter punks killed an off-duty cop. I guess the cop was gay. He took the punks to a hotel in Jersey to party, and they cut him up. Then they took his car and drove to Tompkins and double-parked. Within a minute, cops were swarming out of nowhere, and the kids got arrested. One of them ended up escaping from the Jersey Youth Facility and came back to the park again.

They busted him on Avenue A.

At this point in my life, crack has caught up with me. About a year ago, I was smoking up on 23rd street, and I just started hearing voices of people who were trying to kill me. I was running like a maniac in a movie, stopping traffic, opening doors, screaming, "Help me, let me in, please!" The cops were all over me. I jumped on the bus, and then ran off the back into a church. I thought the priest was going to set me up for murder. The police surrounded me with a SWAT team. They had sharp shooters and everything in case I was gonna take a hostage.

A few months ago, I was smoking crack on 13th Street. I bugged out and ran into a bodega and locked myself in the meat freezer. I tore up all the food in there—major damage. Then somebody was jiggling the door, and I said, I'm gonna bust through these fuckers. I ran out screaming, and the cops wrestled me and put on the cuffs. They sent me to a clinic. It's so embarrassing. Now, I've got to take Respitol and Zoloft for depression. If I smoke even a little bit of crack I'll lose my mind.

As I get older, living on the street loses its appeal. I used to have friends out here, and some of them are still here, but now I'm mostly alone. I was sleeping out in Greenwich Village a couple months ago, and some kids kicked me in my head. There was like eleven of them, and I had to fight my way out. One of my friends got his back lit on fire while he was sleeping. He's got terrible scars all across his back. There's a lot of other people out here who drink themselves to death.

The people on these benches are laughing and joking, but their life is hell. They're just waiting for the grim reaper. I've been in programs with a lot of these guys. None of us stuck with it, but I'm only 33.

I still have time. I'm tired of it. I can't spend another ten years out here. It's not fun. You're just scheming to get ten dollars so you can get a bag of garbage. It ain't even real dope. Half this stuff is crushed up pills.

I have one friend who got clean, and now he's after his life long dream of hiking the Appalachian Trail. He's walking the whole thing. That kind of inspired me to get it together. The only way to do that was move back to my mom. If I called her she wouldn't want to believe a word of it, so I had to show her that I was clean.

Two weeks ago I just went up there and knocked on her door. She didn't have the heart to turn me away. I've been off dope for about three weeks, and crack for a couple months. I can't drink beer anymore, because I've got acid reflux disease. If I drink one or two beers, I'm sick. It's like God stopped me.

If I went to college, my life would be much different now. If I had that piece of paper, I could bounce back. Most of the people who do well at rehab programs are those who have the skills to get back on their feet financially. When you sit around broke, you're depressed. That depression makes you want to say fuck it. Next dollar I get, I'm getting high.

Even though I don't have college, I do have some intelligence going for me. I just took the Civil Service Exam, and I got a ninety-eight, an eighty-eight with an extra ten points for being a veteran. My only roadblock from getting a state job is my misdemeanors. I'm going to try to go down to the courthouse and get that taken care of.

I just applied for a job as a nurse's aide. I got a new pair of slacks, a tie, and some shirts. I just got to get a new pair of shoes—some Oxfords. I like them Oxfords. You know, what the policemen wear. I like dressing clean, a nice haircut. Once you grow up with good home training, you never lose it.

Do you think that this is the last time you're going to have to kick?

Yeah. I don't want to die. My heart isn't good. I can feel it in my arms and legs. It's like tension. Every time they put me on EKG they say I've had many heart attacks.

I need to be focused. The man that you see now is not the same man that I used to be when I was drinking. I couldn't even hold a conversation with you. I was obnoxious and angry. I really hope I get that job, because I want to have another kid. That's my next mission in life. I wanna be in the baby's life. I just don't wanna be a sperm donor. I wanna go to ball games, fishing, riding bikes . . .

As our interview comes to a close, I hand James a ten-dollar bill and tell him to make sure that he spends it right. For three months I don't see him in the park, which is a good sign. Finally, in November I call the phone number for his mother's house to request a follow up interview. The voice of an elderly woman answers.

"James Carter? No he doesn't live here. He's a homeless person."

I ask the woman if she knows whether James had entered a program or was living in a shelter. She has not spoken to him in months and has no idea of his where-abouts.

Skunk
New Mexico 1977

photo Skunk

This kid named Critter licked my dog's asshole the other day. I don't know what's wrong with him. We do a lot of dumb shit like that. Sometimes, we'll get all the homeless kids to make retarded noises when people walk by. UMMMM UUMMMM. I can't imagine what they're thinking.

I first meet Skunk late one night in July as the park is about to close. I follow her as she picks up her dog Gargamel's leash and pushes a shopping cart down St. Marks to Astor Place. She proceeds with upbeat confidence as her words flow in a staccato stream of raised inflection.

My mom gave birth to me in a trailer. We were on welfare. My dad was this really controlling asshole who wouldn't even let my mother out of the house. When we were really young, he molested me and my brother. When I was five, my mom got a divorce and my father came after her with a gun. He's crazy. I have like twenty half brothers and sisters that I haven't met, because he's had so many wives. He comes from a fucked up family too. His father, my grandfather, is the leader of the KKK or something.

My relationship with my dad made it really hard for me to trust men. Like if a woman I had just met asked me inside her apartment, I'd do it. But with a guy, no way. I'm straight and everything, I just have a hard time trusting guys.

I had a brother and a sister, and I guess we were

just really fucked up kids. I was always fighting. My mom didn't know what to do with me so I went to a lot of government group homes and treatment centers for "social disorders." They put us on medication and made us get therapy. They said I had a problem dealing with authority, and I was only acting out for attention. It was basically brainwashing. They said if I kept on going the way I was going I'd end up pregnant and on heroin.

I never did use heroin, but I did get pregnant. I was like fifteen at the time and at first I wanted to go through with it. After two months I got morning sickness really bad. It wasn't just in the morning, it lasted all day. My mom gave me some information about abortions, and I had one. She still let me make my own choice, but I'm glad she helped me like that. The guy I was dating was a real asshole about it and told everybody. We broke up.

I was really smart. When I took the IQ test, I was higher than my mom, but I never really got excited about school. They just teach you a bunch of pointless stupid shit. People always made fun of me. I was the only girl with a mohawk and there were only like six other punks. One day in tenth grade, all the jocks decided to throw eggs at me. I went to the principal's office and told him. He just told me to take my dog collar off. I got really pissed and walked out. I never went back.

Right after that, I moved in with this new guy and ended up dating him. I got a job telemarketing and eventually got enough money to get my own place. I started taking care of my own finances, but I was still really dependent on this guy for my self-esteem. I dated him for like two years. He just started acting like more and more of a dick. I had to call the cops on him a few times, because he was choking me.

Eventually I decided I don't need this asshole. Before I left, he was begging me not to go and saying how much he loved me. Then he killed my cat.

While I was living on my own, my mother remarried and moved to Seattle. She didn't have any friends out there, so she wanted me to come. I said OK and hopped on a bus. It was cool for a while, but my step dad was like this straight-laced businessman type. He said that I was a bad influence on his daughter. I didn't want to cause any static, so I went down to Florida to visit my old friend Amy.

Amy had a messed-up childhood just like me. Her dad shot her mom while she was in the room when she was like twelve. She's smart as hell, but she did a lot of dumb shit. She was on heroin when I came down, and I tried to help her kick the habit. That was pretty difficult, but she's clean now. She just had a baby in May.

After I'd been in Florida for six months, I decided it was time to move on. I met a guy named Robert, who drove me and my friend Michelle up to South Carolina. One night Michelle found five hundred dollars in the bathroom of a subway. We bought jewelry and ecstasy and partied like crazy in Myrtle Beach. Before I left, I tried out for the MTV show *Fear*. They gave me a video interview, and they really liked me. I hope they email me back.

After a few weeks, Robert drove me and Michelle to New York. That was two months ago. New York is cool because there's a lot of other homeless kids here. When I was staying in Florida, I was the only young person. The rest were just scary home bums. It was really hard to panhandle there. But here you can panhandle all day and never ask the same person twice. There's also a pretty strong sense of community. When I first came in, lots of kids showed me where to go get food and where to sleep. There's a lot of hookups for the homeless in New York.

There's definitely a lot of punks here. There's two kinds: house punks, which are punks that live in a house, and crusty punks or gutter punks who live on the street. I guess I'm a crusty punk. There are some house punks who look down on us and won't hang out because we're dirty, but there are also house punks who'll let you come over to their place and shower. I have a group of about five other kids who I hang out with. We keep all of our shit in the same shopping cart. There's a few changes of clothes, some dog food, and a carpet to sleep on.

The cops here are pretty tough. I've gotten two tickets so far, both bullshit. One was for disorderly conduct. The cop said I was blocking the sidewalk, but I was just sitting up against a building. The other was for aggressive begging. I was just sitting there asking people for change. I wasn't bothering them. The cop was a real asshole. He told me to go back to Washington. I'm supposed to go to court August 9th, but I think I'm going to leave New York by then. But all the cops aren't assholes. One cop gave me a dollar and a can of dog food.

It's hard to find a place to sleep at night, so I usually stay up until five or six in the morning. Then we go to sleep in the park. I panhandle at least a few hours a day. My friends usually get some beer money, but I don't even drink. I tried it once, but I don't like being around drunk people. It makes you lose control of your body, and it impairs your judgment. Other drugs don't really do that. I still smoke pot and drop acid or X. Today when I was panhandling, some guy kicked us down a joint. That was all right.

A few weeks ago, I met this guy who paid us

money to walk on him. It was the weirdest thing. He'll lie on his back and tell us to jump on his crotch. I don't really know what the guy's deal is, but we made sixty dollars in like an hour. He says he works for Howard Stern. Yesterday, this guy came up to me and Michelle while we were panhandling and gave us both a dollar. He said that he paid for massages. I asked him if he wanted a back rub. He said no, my dick. That was freaky, but he just walked away. Overall the people have been all right. I haven't had anybody steal anything or threaten me.

My current situation has its ups and downs just like anything. Overall, I'm pretty happy. If I didn't like what I was doing I could go get a job and an apartment. I'm just out for lots of different experiences. From the time I left my asshole boyfriend I've definitely become a stronger person. I used to think that I wasn't worth anything, because I was in treatment centers and I was weird. Now I just don't care about what people think. I used to put makeup on everyday, because I thought people wouldn't like me if I didn't. Now I don't give a shit. You either like me for who I am or you don't like me at all. I used to think that I needed a guy to validate myself, but I haven't been in a relationship for over a year now. I figure that it's better to be by myself. I'm still figuring shit out.

Everything is a learning experience, even bad things. I like to learn about everything. I guess you could say I'm on a spiritual journey. I'm definitely not enlightened, but I have figured a few things out. I don't really believe in a god or a hell. When I go to churches to eat, they give you pamphlets. It's like they can't be OK with you unless you join their little club.

Now that I'm older I get along with my mother much better. She singing in this band up in Seattle, so she's been exploring herself artistically. She's a real spiritual person. When I was a kid, I really hated her, but now we have a good relationship. I try to call her collect whenever I can. She's kind of worried about me, and she always asks me if I've gotten the traveling out my system. She wants to see me go to college and succeed. She's like a friend.

I spend a lot of my time drawing. I love to draw. I designed this alien tattoo on my leg. See? I can do graphic arts work with 350 printing presses. I'm great with computers. You wouldn't think it by looking at me, but I'm pretty smart. Do you want to look at my scrapbook?

Skunk sorts through her shopping cart and removes a bound diary of pasted pictures, keepsakes, and drawings. She flips through and offers an explanation of each page:

This is a picture of my friends from Florida.

I took this Women sign from an abandoned bank I was squatting in.

This is a pamphlet from a Mumia Abu Jamal protest I went to last summer.

This next page is one of my poems:

In my haste, thinking I see change,
I spend all dreaming,
thinking of what could be,
yet unsure of myself
    and still a little frightened at each corner.
I walk this twisted path a silent mourner.
I won't look you in the eye,
because then my soul will be exposed.
What will happen next, I don't know,
I'm just along for the ride.

But once you know me please don't run and hide.
I wish someone would understand me
instead of feeling awkward.
The years just go by and still I'm misunderstood.
I want to make change.
I want to help someone have a better life.
I want you to open your eyes and see the world.
I want for everyone to be free.
Before any of that, I have to know myself.
What if I'm not what I want to be?
Then what the fuck?

      Embrace yourself and dream of change.
      Dream, dream, dream. I love to dream.

Tom Brokaw with 666 on his forehead.

This is a pamphlet from the Twelve Tribes. They're this weird cult we met in Fort Myers who wanted us to come live in the woods with them.

I used to have bi hawks, two little mowhawks. *(points to two pieces of hair taped on the page)*

This is a condom from a college campus.

Some Christian band gave us this sticker.

I've got Greyhound ticket stubs.

These are pictures of a driveway party where everybody got naked.

This is a picture of Allison. I wrote bitch ho next to her, because she tried to steal my dog.

I have Marky Ramone's autograph.

I have the old safety pin from my bra.

My dog's baby fang.

This next page is an anarchist manifesto.

This is a picture of me getting my piercings. They really hurt when you get them, but tattoos are worse. I have seven. I think they look pretty. It's art.

This is a poem written by my friend Shadow after one of our friends committed suicide:

Looking up at the ledge as my feet tumble above me.
I'm dizzy, drowsy.
My death defying fall will release my truth.
The only truth ever known.
The ultimate release.
Relieved of life.

Suicides of the selfish
only insure the survival of us,
the survivors.

The next one is a picture of when we smeared poop all over a McDonald's drive-through window. I guess we were really big on poop for a few days.

This is Mental Mike, this old hippie guy who lives with his mom.

I have some pamphlets on how to shoot heroin. I don't do heroin, but I liked the pamphlet.

This is the Jack is gay page. He stole my dog from me, so I took his picture and glued all these ads for gay sex from the *Village Voice* on top of it.

Here's an upside-down crucifix. I don't worship Satan. I just make fun of all religion.

A lot of people don't understand this way of life, and they're afraid of it. People might look at me on the street, and because of the way I look, they'll assume that I'm trash, or an addict, or a thief. You can't judge people like that. I love to walk up and talk to somebody who looks down on me. It's like I can totally squash all of their misconceptions. I've got a good head on my shoulders.

George
Okinawa, Japan 1974

Dressed in a neat collared shirt, and a clean pair of slacks, George appears strangely out of place amongst his disheveled compatriots on Crusty Lane. His clean-shaven face and alert mannerisms are more indicative of an NYU student than someone who spends his nights sleeping in East River Park.

I was born on a small air force base in Japan. My mother was only eighteen. She was an undercover narcotics officer for the military police, and my father was an Airborne Ranger. I spent most of my time with a Korean nanny named Ko. I spent so much time with her that some of my first words were Korean. "Edi wah jah say oh." Come here now.

When I was two, we got transferred to San Francisco. My mother bounced around quite a bit, because whenever she made a bust, they'd transfer her so she'd be safe. I don't really remember too much about Frisco, because I was always in the apartment. They had to keep me under surveillance because of my mother's line of work. There was always a possibility that one of the dealers would try to snatch me up to keep my mother from testifying. I got escorted everywhere by CIDs *(Criminal Investigation Division)*. They even had a private teacher come in for school.

My parents split up after we'd been in Frisco for a while. My dad had a serious case of post-traumatic stress disorder after being in Vietnam. He was just very volatile. He wasn't a drinker, and he didn't get high, but his mood was like nitroglycerin. You couldn't shake him up. All of this I know from my mother, because I was really too young to remember him.

The next move was Fort Sill, Oklahoma. It was great. They let me go to the regular school on the base, because my mother wasn't an MP anymore. It was a pretty good time for me. I got to do all the fun kid stuff—Scooby Doo peal and stick tattoos, super heroes, making out with girls. I remember jumping off the parking garage with a bag over my head thinking it would act like a parachute. I broke my foot, but it actually worked out pretty good for me, because I got to get out of school for a while. My birthday was coming up, but since I wasn't in school I was worried nobody would come to the party. My mom passed out these flyers to both first-grade classes. Sixty kids ended up showing up. I got a shitload of presents. It was sick. I still have the pictures of me with all the cute first-grade girls.

At Fort Sill my mother started getting really close with this guy named Jack. At first he'd just come to parties. Then he'd start showing up for dinner. I guess it didn't really bother me, because Jack was a cool guy. He made sure that I got picked up from school and taught me how to ride a bike and shit. He just fell into place.

When I was nine, my mother left the military and married Jack. We moved out to this little one-street-light town called Skawkonda in southern Illinois. I adjusted pretty quick. Being in the country was great. It was all about Cub Scouts and fishing and stuff. I met a lot of friends. Then Jack started to beat my mother. I remember one time when they were fighting, I pulled his shotgun on him. That was the end of that.

After my mom left Jack, we moved in with her sister-in-law in Chicago. It was a rough transition, because I wasn't used to the way city kids acted. We were living in this huge apartment complex that was predominantly Hispanic, and here I was this little white country boy.

One night right after we moved, I woke up in the middle of the night and found my mom and my aunt pulling bong hits in the living room. A few days later I found out that she was taking speed. I didn't say anything about it, but it really changed the way I thought about her. Before that I thought that my mom was super strong, but now I started to worry.

When I first got to Chicago, I spent a lot of time inside the apartment playing with my aunt's turntables. I didn't really fit in at school at all. Nobody would talk to me. One day I was at my locker, and I was looking at this really hot chick across the hall. I smiled at her, and her boyfriend caught it. He started a big scene, and then these three guys from a gang called The Vice Lords just started pummeling me.

That night, my mom brought me over to the apartment next door. This kid from school, Javier, lived there with his father. (Later I found out that my mom was dealing speed to the guy.) My mom made me tell Javier's father how I got beat up. Then she talked to the guy for a while and asked if it was OK for me to stay with him and Javier for the weekend.

Javier like totally accepted me. He took me out and introduced me to his friends. I was hanging out, and they got me drunk for the very first time. Then they took me to a house party. I was just standing against the wall. The next day Javier's friends taught me how to dance, and I was able to do a couple steps. People were like, "Hey, white boy can dance!"

Javier gave me the lowdown about the city. He taught me lit. Lit is that which is real. He was dropping serious lit, and putting me down with my surroundings. That weekend really changed my whole outlook on Chicago.

That Monday I was waiting for the bus, and Javier's friend Xavier pulled up in a car. I got in and we drove into school. When we got inside, he told me to point out the kids who beat me up. As soon as I did, Xavier just snapped his fingers, and like fifteen dudes came out of the woodwork and beat the living shit out of these kids. That was the last time I had any problems in school.

I started hanging out with Javier's friends pretty regular, and I came to rely less on my mom. That was when I started getting wild. At the end of my freshman year, I was walking to this juice bar called Medusa's, and I saw these guys shooting dice on the opposite corner. I got halfway through the street, and somebody yelled, "Fuck all y'all muthafuckas!" I heard a car fishtail, and then I saw this flashing light. Ba-da-da-da-da-da! They got sprayed with a Tek 9. I got hit by a stray bullet. It bounced off my ribs and went down into my liver.

I was laid up for a while, so I had to spend a lot of time inside the apartment with my mom. That kind of put a strain on our relationship. She'd just be sitting on the couch smoking weed, vegging out, and gaining weight. We fought all the time. Sometimes she'd catch me smoking weed, and she'd scream at me. But it was like, she had a bong and her own weed. She'd smoke it right at the kitchen table. She'd even ask me to go buy weed for her.

When I got better, I wasn't the same. I quit giving a shit about school, and I quit giving a shit about my mom. One night I told her that I was going over to a friend's house, and she said, "The fuck you are." That just blew up into a big argument. I ended up walking out the door, and I didn't come back.

I hung out with a lot of different friends for like a month. One night, there was snow on the ground, and I was really drunk. I left this house party and walked into the adjoining apartment building and passed out in the stairwell. Somebody that was leaving for work called the cops, and the officer put me in the car and took me back to my mother's house. When we got there, my mother said, "Keep him." The cops wouldn't let me go unless my mother signed these papers. I was really pissed. I put all my stuff in a duffel bag, and they took me to a group home.

I stayed there for like three days. Then they transferred me to my first foster home. After like two days, they put me in another foster home. I went through seven foster homes in like a three-week period. It was just emergency temporary placements. They all wanted babies that they could mold. Nobody wanted a fucked up fourteen-year-old. I wasn't hostile to these people. I just wasn't what they were looking for. While that was happening, I ended up getting totally removed from the school system.

After my seventh placement, I met this skater kid named Reggie. He took me home for dinner once, and he introduced me to his mother. She was this nice old church-going lady, and she was totally flabbergasted about my situation. She called up social services and asked if she could keep me. They sent somebody to check out her place so she could apply for a temporary license. I stayed there for a while. It was OK.

They put me in an alternative school for problem kids. That kind of sucked, because I wasn't really a disruptive kid. I just hated homework. This new school was junk. It was so easy that I'd finish all my work in like an hour and go to sleep for the day or read a book. I went through a lot of books.

When I walked home from the bus, I always used to see this racecar parked in one of the neighbor's garages. After I walked by it a few times, I finally got the guts to go up and talk to the guy working on it. He poked his head out and asked me to hand him a wrench. Then he gave me a welding mask, and I got to watch him weld. They guy's name was Charlie. He was a building a circle dirt track car with a V8. I started asking him a bunch of questions, and he invited me in for dinner. We had steak, and his wife had these great bottles of cream soda. I haven't been able to find them since then. I think it's like a local distributor. Anyway, I stopped off at Charlie's a lot after school, and he taught me how to mig and tig weld. I learned how to rebuild a V8. He even let me drive his Firebird. Charlie taught me a lot about work ethic.

I stayed there for a few months, but when summer hit, social services pulled me out of Reggie's house, because they wouldn't give his mom a license. That sucked, because Charlie was starting to take me to races to be on his pit crew. I was also going to church, and I sort of had a girlfriend. It was a good life, but I had to leave.

Social Services told me that I could either go to this group home called Gateway or I could go on a thirty-day adventure course canoeing though Minnesota. They kind of built up the canoe thing, and I decided to give it a shot.

It was great. I loved it. We went for hundreds of miles into Canada. I was king of the one-match fire. I even pulled this one kid out of the river who couldn't swim. I came out of it eight pounds heavier, suntanned like a motherfucker, and I had made a lot of good friends. After that they put me in this place called Arrow Head Ranch in Southern Illinois. It was an all-male facility out in the country. It was all right. We had six groups of twelve guys and we'd play sports and shit. We were actually the only team to score a goal against the Korean Group Home Soccer team. We beat them 2-1. I was right inside midfielder.

About fourteen months into Arrow Head, I got called up to the main office. They said that my aunt Beth was trying to get all of this information about me, and they needed my signature to release it. I got on the phone and talked to her.

I hadn't talked to my Aunt Beth since I was five. Apparently, she had spoken to my mother, and she freaked out when she heard she'd given up custody. After my eighteen months passed, I moved down with my aunt in Maryland. It was kind of weird, because my aunt was like my mother's twin sister. But, unlike my mom, she ended up being really cool. It was really stable. She owns her own accounting company, so the house was nice. It was me, my aunt, my uncle and my two little cousins, Jenny and Steven. It was cool, because I got to be a big brother. My aunt even let me borrow her car.

When I got out of Arrowhead, I had all the credits that I needed to graduate high school, but my aunt wanted me to go to a regular school for a while. It was cool. I was doing my own thing, dressing real nice— didn't even wear tennis shoes. I guess the preppy thing worked, 'cause I finally got laid.

I'd drink sometimes on the weekends, but this time I kept it in check. When I graduated high school in '92, my Aunt got me this job working for a company called Yusevi International. We imported Middle Eastern artifacts. I did pretty good there, and I got promoted to stock supervisor. Then my aunt helped me score this awesome job at a place called The Silver

Star Group. We would buy out small businesses that were failing and restart them with different management. The boss put me in charge of a yogurt shop in a mall. My aunt helped me out with a lot of the accounting aspects. There was a lot of work, but it paid awesome. I got my own apartment in a private community on the Chesapeake Bay. After a while, I put a down payment on my own condo in Aberdeen and I took out a loan on a '97 Prelude with all sorts of bells and whistles. They delivered it on Christmas Day.

I still hadn't talked to my mother for nine years. I decided that I was going to take some time off from work and go visit her in Chicago. From there I was going to drive her to Cancun and we were going to have a talk. On January 24th I came home from work, and my aunt was in my apartment crying. I asked her what was wrong. She told me that she just got a phone call. My mother shot herself.

What! I tripped out. I took a flight out to Chicago the next day. It was suspicious circumstances, but they said that she took a bullet to the stomach from her own hand. I didn't have any brothers or sisters, so I had to put on the funeral. There were a lot of people there I didn't know. I kicked everybody out at one point so I could have some time alone in the viewing room with her. She didn't look like my mom. She was fat and all white. I bawled like a three-year-old.

That's the worst thing to happen to me in my whole life. It still affects me to this day. I hate her for it. I hate the fact that I didn't get in contact with her sooner. I think maybe part of the reason she killed herself was because I never tried to find her. I've got guilt that won't go away. I could have called her, but I chose not to because I was angry. That's my fault.

I had to take a month off from work, but I still wasn't ready to come back to such a tough job. I sold my car and my condo, and I moved into a room for rent. Instead of driving, I bought a bicycle.

I was really depressed. I mostly just sat in my apartment doing nothing. Then I started taking some classes at a community college, and I met a lot of rave kids. I had been a little bit of a DJ ever since Chicago, and these kids thought my tapes were cool. I got to spin out some raves. That was a huge release, and it helped me forget. I started partying hard, real hard—lots of coke, crazy ecstasy. People kicked me down a lot of drugs, because I spun.

I didn't care. I still don't care. I just wanted to be numb and have a good time. I moved in with a couple rave kids in Thompson and made some spare cash working for a coke dealer. After a month or so I met this girl who kind of fell for me. She was cool. She did my laundry and stuff. We fucked and hung out at the raves. Then a year and a half ago, I found out that she was stripping. That pissed me off, and we fought about that. Then my money started coming up missing, and people started stealing my coke. I got in a huge fight with my girlfriend, and said fuck it. I packed my shit up and went to Brooklyn. It was just a spur of the moment thing, but I guess it was mostly because I knew I could make a lot of money dealing in the rave scene.

I rented a room on Fifth Ave in Park Slope and started selling ecstasy at raves. I had a connection who would drop like a thousand pills on me, and it was no problem getting rid of it. After five months of going to raves, I met this cute Puerto Rican chick. She took me over to her place and she shot a bag of heroin. I said fuck it, and I got high too. Pretty soon, I was shooting like a hundred dollars a day. I started going down to Tompkins Square a lot to cop, and I met a lot of the kids. Sometimes I'd take people from the park to stay at my apartment. Eventually I couldn't afford the rent anymore, so I just put all my stuff in a backpack and headed out to live in East River Park. It really didn't bother me, because I've camped out in the woods with wolves and snakes. There's always a lot of people camping out down there, so nobody really bothers us.

For a few weeks I stayed with this stripper who lives in a hotel down on the Bowery. We had a falling out, because she thought I stole something from her. One thing about me is that I don't steal. I have a work ethic. I bust my ass for my money. I don't even spange.

In July I called up 411 and got in touch with my friend Henry in Montreal. He was really glad to hear from me and invited me to come visit. I said, "Listen, when I come up, I'm going to be sick for a while." Henry said that I could sleep on his couch while I detoxed. When I hopped off the plane, I started throwing up all over the place. When we got back to Henry's place, he cut me up a couple lines of X to take the edge off. I was an utter bear. I don't know how he stood me, but after a while I started eating and I felt alright.

Henry let me borrow some of his old turntables, and I started mixing. I made some tapes and passed them around. Henry's friends really liked it, and asked me to spin out at some parties. It was awesome, I'd party at night, and ski during the day. I put back a lot of weight and put some money in the bank.

When I heard that the World Trade Center went down, I wanted to go back to New York to check on my friends. I just got back three days ago. I was hoping that I could stay with one of my friends on Avenue B, but I haven't seen him around. So far I've smoked a little bit of weed since I've got back, but I'm clean, and I'm not fucking around.

Right now I'm hanging out in the park, because I know the kids, and we get along. I'm definitely not a crusty punk. They don't have any real goals, and they really don't want to be anywhere. You can't really have any self-esteem if you beg for money all day long. A lot of those guys will suck a guy's dick for dope money. I don't want to be a piece of meat like that. I'm not saying that there's a big difference between me and them, but at least I've still got my pride. I won't let myself get to that point.

Two weeks after our interview I see George shooting up in East River Park. His appearance has deteriorated, and his words trickle out in a lethargic quiver. A month later I see him walking out of a bodega on Avenue A. He tells me that he had secured a job as a delivery person, moved into a friend's apartment, and is no longer shooting dope.

I don't see George through the winter. One morning in April of 2002 I speak to one of his close friends in the park.

George died of a heroin overdose in February.

photo Jeff Owen

The Lighter Side of Crusty Lane

Cheyenne, Wyoming
James Osborne

So there I was on this double container, a hotshot from Eugene to Kansas City. The night before we were running from the bulls, ducking in and out of bushes. I didn't know it at the time, but I had totally covered myself in poison ivy. By the time we got to Cheyenne it itched like you wouldn't fucking believe. I was like, I have to get this shit checked out. I told my two friends I'd meet 'em by noon the next day at the North Platt Railroad Yard. Then I bailed out on the fly.

As soon as I got to the highway, some guy picked me up and took me to the hospital. I can't pay my bills, so I told the receptionist that my name was Richard Ledbetter. After four hours of sitting in the waiting room the doctor gave me a prescription for these pills and this lotion. That kinda sucked, because I didn't have any way to pay for it. But when I came out, I bumped into the guy who gave me the ride, and he took me to a pharmacy and bought it for me. After that he took me to a pizza joint, and then he left me with a twenty-dollar bill.

First thing I did was buy a pack of smokes. Now I had been jumping trains for the last three days, and as soon as that nicotine hit me I felt this unbelievable shit coming on. It was terrible I can't even explain it.

I'm walking like a duck, practicing La Maze breathing techniques so I can keep it in. I would have just gone around the corner, but I figured that being that it was Cheyenne, the cops would just immediately arrest me. Finally it all just came loose all fucking everywhere. I went behind this dumpster and tried to clean myself off, but it was all soupy and sticking. The only paper I had was the prescription receipt, so I took it out and wiped it up the best I could.

As I'm putting my pants back on, I see this guy coming down the road with a big backpack. He was normal looking, but obviously a traveler. I asked him if he had any shorts that I could borrow. He was like, "I'll sell you my lucky drawers for ten dollars." Then he took out this tiny ass pair of jogging shorts. I finally talked him down to four dollars.

I took the shorts and walked down to this creek and stripped down. As soon as I got into the middle of the stream two cops pulled up. I had nothing on but my hat and my glasses. They were like, "What the fuck are you doing boy?" I told them what happened, and they just looked at me with a straight face and said, "You got any drugs in this bag, boy?" They opened up my bag, and found the medicine. They told me that since I couldn't produce a Richard Ledbetter ID, I needed to show them the receipt. I was screwed!

The cops took both bottles and told me that if they caught me by the river again, they were gonna arrest me. I couldn't finish cleaning the shit off my pants, so I had to put on the Nike shorts that this guy had sold me. They were like spandex. So I walk ten miles down the road looking like a homeless Richard Simmons.

Anyway, after that nobody would give me a ride, and I had to spend the night in the bushes. I rolled into North Platt the next day at 2 o'clock, and some guy in the yard told me that my friends just left.

So yeah, you were asking about what this lifestyle has taught me. I guess I've learned a lot of things, and some other things I'm still figuring out. But I do know this: Never shit yourself in Cheyenne, Wyoming.

Prophet (right) with friend, Boner
pofsin666@yahoo.com

I lived in this neighborhood my whole life. After my mom kicked me out of the house, I was out on the street for awhile. This Christian preacher helped me find a place in a squat called Dos Blockos. I thought it was awesome because I slept on the top floor—the penthouse. It was like a family. I remember when the city was getting ready to take over the building, all the squatters in the neighborhood were out on the street trying to fight it. We had the door welded shut, and we put these metal spikes on the roof so they couldn't land helicopters. It was so beautiful. That was our castle, our fortress.

I was sitting up in my room with my friends, and I was crying. I had my knife in my hand, and if anybody came in, I was gonna to use it. The priest came in and talked to me, and eventually he got me to put the knife down. We went to his church, then we came back the next day. It was so beautiful to see all my people there on the street. Dos Blockos is gone, but I'll never forget what it was like to be a part of that family.

Prophet is currently working on a screenplay titled Silent Tears.

Mumbly Joe

Shit, man, I don't know. I just wanna have a job and a place and a dog, and just crash. Nothing much, just a little bit of food in the fridge. I'd rather work for my money. I really would. I go up to Maine for blueberry harvest, and I'm going to Massachusetts for cranberries, but I don't know how to go about something like that in New York.

Doug

We go to towns and wonder why we're there.

Leroy

I just did this my whole life, and I don't know no other way to be. I'm looked down on, but I'm not worried about what other people think. I just live by the day.

Bayne

In front of a mosaic on St. Marks Place by street artist Jim Power

I ran away from home a couple times when I was younger, and after a while, I ended up staying out here. I went down the wrong track a couple times, but I've learned a lot. I've seen a lot of things. As you get older, you get younger. I'm thirty-two, but I still feel like I'm twenty-four.

K

I was born in Poland, and my family came here for political asylum when I was six. I didn't speak English, so it was horrible. By the time I got to high school, I realized that I was a completely different person than the others, so I got used to it. My parents were all into punk themselves, so this lifestyle just kind of came naturally. My dad shaved my head for the first time.

Being on the road makes me feel whole. It's a sense of reality that I don't experience when I'm between four walls. I've learned who I am and where I belong. I've learned that appearances don't matter. Even the most dirty, scary-looking people can have the most loving hearts in the whole world.

Heather MacKay (right) with Erik

grimace60@hotmail.com

"To those who didn't know the man, rest in peace. Kill for Grimace tonight."

My dog Grimace just died a few months ago. He was my man for seven years. Just about the smartest dog you've ever seen. I got this tattoo on my neck the day after they put him down. The G and the R hurt like a bitch, but after that my nerves were so dull that I didn't feel the rest. He'll be eight next month.

Phoenix Mercury

Phoenixmercuryrising@yahoo.com

Phoenix Mercury was born and raised in the Lower East Side. This is a section from his rap "Can You See Hear and Feel."

I be the alien lurking
on the East Side.
Or maybe that angel
from the downside.
Or that creature
that lurks in the dark night,
or that schizophrenic
imprisoned by his own mind.
Let me go. Let G glow.
Let me flow. Let me fly.
Let me be bouncing off these walls in my distorted fantasies.
A painted reality. A monstrosity, embedded in my anatomy.
I can feel something sharp lodged in my arteries.
I guess it could be the loss of my family. . . .

Fu and Natasha
aboynamedfu@hotmail.com
ciderpunk7@hotmail.com

I've never been in love with anyone else before, and I've never known love until I met my wife. I don't think I ever would have known if she hadn't shown me what it was. I'd rather be out here on the street with her than anywhere else without her.

Ditto. *(giggle)*

Oscar
noderailers@hotmail.com

I may be lying in the gutter, but I'm staring at the stars.

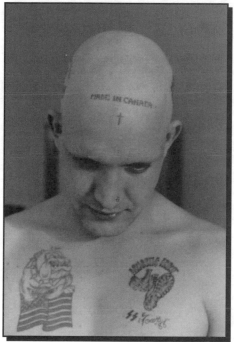

photo Clayton Patterson

Frenchy the Scamp, c. 1988. RIP, 2002

Dan

It's the adventure, not knowing what's ahead of you. I started to enjoy it more and more as I got used to it. When I'm out here, I always got somebody to talk to. I can change it at any time. My future's up to me, pretty much.

Monte
supertrampdb@yahoo.com

My stepdad used to beat me up, but by the time I got to be fourteen, I got big enough to fight back. One day I beat him up, and he told me to leave. I was like OK. I moved in with some squatters, and they taught me how to live. I been riding freight trains for three years. I just go wherever I fucking feel like. We don't stay anywhere for more than a month and a half.

Silver Fish
silver_fish_22@hotmail.com

I been traveling for about four years. I actually went to college for a year, but I got kicked out. That was fine with me, I didn't want to go to college anyway, but when I turned eighteen somebody told me that a relative had left money for me to go to college on. I tried it, but it wasn't for me.

My generation is fucked up. So many people are trying to get ahead wanting more, more, more. They all watch TV and buy all sorts of stupid shit. When you get done making payments on your car, you start making payments on your house. It just seems like a trap. It doesn't seem that a lot of people think for themselves.

I gained a lot of self confidence from departing from that world. When I was in high school, I thought that I had to do all the things that were expected of me. Like if you're a girl you have to try to be pretty. You have to be smart, but not so smart that it's intimidating. Out here it's expected for girls to be tougher. Most of the guys aren't looking for somebody who's dumb and pretty. They want something real. A lot of kids in this lifestyle know what's up.

In September Silver Fish left New York to harvest cranberries in Massachusetts.

Max

rattkiler@hotmail.com

I was born in Rumania. I came to the United States because you didn't really have options under the Communist Party. There was a lot of repression and a lot of bullshit. If you played punk music or dressed like a punk, the government would take you and your family away.

I've been traveling for about eight years. I stay out here, because I'm insane. They told me I was manic depressive with social anxiety disorder. I can't adjust to society worth a fuck. Sometimes I feel like I can't be normal. Maybe I'll find a girl to get me straight, and maybe I'll die on the railroad tracks. I don't really care.

Rafa

I used to go to Catholic school on 10th Street, and after school I used to come down to East River Park in my little uniform. When I was like fourteen I started living with my boyfriend, and I wasn't allowed in my mom's house, so I crashed down here a lot.

I feel like I was born in the wrong time and place. Back in the days you could go to unknown places to see unknown faces. Genuine adventure was the norm. Now all these people are consumed by security. I like to have genuine experiences.

Crystal

I left home at fifteen. There were a lot of traveling kids who came through my town, and they seemed a lot more free than everybody else. I met Anaconda a few years ago. We've got together and broken up a few times, but being on the road has really brought us closer. We rely on each other more.

Anaconda briefly looks up from a video game on a cell phone of unknown origin. He nods in agreement.

Jo Jo Dancer
jojo666rca@aol.com

I didn't see eye to eye with my parents, so when I was seventeen, I started hopping freights. I been doing it for five years. I wanted to see what was on the outside. I wanted to find myself. Who knows? This journey might not ever stop.

Sparky
I like to watch out for people.
I like to get lost. One day
I hope to change.

Erik
erikislord@yahoo.com

You can use my real name, cause I'm not afraid of nothing. I'm not a fucking liar, and I'm not a thief. I pride myself on that shit.

SICK
by Chaos

i'm sick of life
sick of trying
sick of cops
and my friends dying
sick of love
sick of hate
sick of realizing things to late
i'm sick of people
sick of god
sick of wondering what lies
beyond
sick of faith
sick of hope...
sick of these thoughts
that plague my brain
suicide
gone insane

*Chaos died of a heroin over-
dose in East River Park in
July of 2002.*

Newlyweds, Doyle and Rachel

The Outskirts

The Tompkins Square community extends far beyond the confines of Crusty Lane and the Living Room. In this section I have included some of the regulars who do not frequent these two locations.

Lawrence LaDouceur
Arlington, Virginia 1950

Freethinking is something that I developed because the education system failed me. When you don't learn according to their instructions, it causes tension in your brain. The potential in my brain is so great that I couldn't grasp the ideas that were presented to me. I was fortunate that I didn't learn, because then I would have developed according to the traditions of society like everybody else. It is because I resisted that I have become the person that I are* today.

Lawrence is the resident prophet of Tompkins Square Park. Although his towering stature makes him hard to forget, few people interact with him directly. He normally avoids company and can usually be found sitting alone on the eastern edge of the park quietly gazing at the world. Although the majority of his interactions are docile and withdrawn, he is occasionally overcome by a surge of inspiration that transforms him into an unrelenting extrovert. The first time that I witness one of these episodes, Lawrence is exuberantly pacing

---

*Lawrence uses the verb "are" with all masculine gender subjects.

through the center of the park, shouting at the crowd of sun-
bathers on the lawn: THE CREATOR CREATED HE.
HE IS MAN AND MALE. HE IS MINIATURE CRE-
ATORS, NOT US. THE CREATOR DIVIDED
THEM INTO SPIRIT, WOMAN, SHE, AND SPIR-
IT, WOMAN, FEMALE, HER. SHE WAS TAKEN
FROM HE, LEAVING HER AND THEY FROZE.
THE CREATOR PURIFIED AND POLARIZED
SPIRIT, CREATING SOUL.

IF YOU KNEW WHAT YOU WERE DOING TO
HER, YOU WOULD STOP!!!

Lawrence is often mocked by testosterone inspired young
males, who only strengthen his resolve to relate his enlightened
convictions. One regular tells me that a drunken reveler once
smashed a board over Lawrence's head. Lawrence stood up
and resumed his oration, oblivious to the perpetrator.

I first sit down to speak with Lawrence in early August.
He seems rather uncomfortable with my attempts to pry into
his past. Instead, he elaborates on his philosophy with fever-
ish enthusiasm.

I first came to Tompkins Square in '93, so that's
really not very long compared to some of the people.
It's a good place, there's a lot of soulful energy. It's
definitely been a very important place for me as far as
developing my philosophy. That first started coming
together about eight years ago when I started smoking a lot of high-grade marijuana. It really opened up
my mind to new ways of thinking that had been closed
off to me because of my limited experience. I really
didn't know I was doing it at the time, but I was laying behind all of my previous misconceptions and dis-
covering my real identity within thoughts that were
my own. Without knowing it, I was on my way to

becoming a philosopher and a prophet.

The first door that I unlocked was overcoming society's misconceptions of God. The Catholicism that I was exposed to early in my development portrayed an image of a God that is removed from humanity. In 1994 I had the realization that the true essence of spirit isn't concentrated in one external God, but it is dispersed throughout everything in creation. There isn't just one God, or source of spirit. That spirit of godliness is everywhere, and every individual is created with that true spirit of virgin virtue. Virgin virtue is our connection with the creator.

We lose virgin virtue because we subject ourselves to the roles that society creates for us. Sons want to identify themselves as he, man, and male, and they want to fulfill society's expectations for that role. They want to be tough and aggressive. They lose their awareness of sensitivity and start to view the daughters as sex objects. The slander, authority and dictatorship that daughters are subject to destroys the virgin virtue of everyone involved, but it's not the daughters that are at fault. Every daughter is innocent, naive and spontaneous, soft and sensitive. Daughters are superior. Sons are inferior.

When we are first conceived, we are given this wonderful identity. We each have the potential to experience depths of emotional sensitivity that are truly awesome. But for most of us, our virgin virtue begins being blocked in the womb. If the parents look upon themselves as sex objects and put all of their attention toward the physical act and not toward the immaculate event, that terrorizes the embryo. Our parents put subconscious thoughts there when we're too young to defend ourselves.

The separation from our true identity continues

and intensifies once we're born. Our whole economy and religious system depends on people who are afraid to think. People rely on a job, or a religious duty to make them feel good and keep busy. They're like sheep. You can't find your true identity until you are ready to ask questions. You can't be afraid to daydream.

We are sensual beings in sensuous bodies. As long as you don't play with the body, you can experience those emotions. Water and dirt make mud. The body is mud. Don't play in the mud. As long as you don't think to touch or be touched, the emotional essence of the relationship increases. It really feels good, because the girl can trust the spirit in the boy. She can radiate her emotion.

I didn't overcome the tension caused by my own emotional dysfunction until I found wedlock. See, I found a daughter in a daydream. When I had time alone, I realized that there was somebody in my daydream with me. She was a real person with real encounters in the present moment. Our relationship is completely non-sexual. My wife possesses me, but I do not possess my wife. Submissive surrender is the way I feel.

My wife was sixteen when we first met back in '93. She's 25 now and it's been a week since we've seen each other. We've never had moments alone together. We've always been in public. One day, maybe we can have that time alone together. That's something to look forward to. I can't divulge where I see my wife, or even my wife's name, because people can hurt others just by thinking about them.

A man and a woman sit down on the bench across from us and begin to engage in a heated argument about sex. Lawrence's face shows an obvious distaste for the subject matter. As the argument reaches a cli-

max, the woman proclaims a sexually explicit com-
ment.*

Oh, I wish people wouldn't talk like that!

*The two combatants ignore his plea, and Lawrence and
I relocate to a different bench.*

I can't stand it when people talk about themselves
with such disrespect! It destroys the emotional
ambiance not only for themselves, but also for everyone around them. The ambiance of quiet brings forward the emotional identity of people. Noise distracts
me from my daydreams.

In daydreaming I've learned everything that I
know. I wonder what I need to know to make my present moment more exact, then I figure things out.
When I have a question, I believe that the answers I
receive are from the creator. You see, reality exists on
more than one plane. There's the basic physical plane
of eating, drinking and sleeping. It's very easy for me
to take care of those basic needs. I used to go to food
kitchens, but now I forage for food. See, the clergy
runs the food kitchens, and they're the ones who teach
the parents to rape the children. I sleep on the street.
I try not to spend too much time worrying about those
needs. If you worry too much about physical pleasure,
your perception can be distorted, and you can deceive
yourself that you are happy when you're not.

I'm better able to explore myself on a spiritual
level living on the street than if I had an apartment
and a job. There's less tension. See you can't predict
when you can experience soulful awareness. A lot of

---

*When reviewing the manuscript, Lawrence insisted that I not reprint the
actual phrase.

people miss those moments, because they're too busy. See, I have the freedom to daydream for as long as I want. I don't have to get up at all. I have the freedom of laying down any time I want. When you have a job you have to follow a schedule. That takes your free thinking away. You can't grow, and you become bored. Those people aren't happy. They don't enjoy life. I are enjoying life.

Lawrence refuses to accept any money for his interview. I don't get a chance to speak to him again until late one evening in March of 2002 as I'm walking over the Williamsburg Bridge.

At first Lawrence doesn't recognize me, but when I remind him of the interview, he thanks me for the opportunity to reflect upon and advance his philosophy. When I ask him where he's been for the last seven months, he tells me that the police around Tompkins Square have grown too troublesome, and in September he was forced to relocate to a vacant lot in Brooklyn.* He is now living in a lean-to made out of plastic tarps and two by fours. Once again, I attempt to pry deeper into Lawrence's past, but he steers me away with his newfound passion for astrology:

I've found the astral plain. That's where the souls go when the body is lifeless. It's where all of the ancients are. The souls up there thought they knew what was right when they were down here. I've communicated with them, and they realized that they didn't know what they thought they knew. Now the astral plain listens to me.

Once we step off the bridge, I ask Lawrence if he wants

---

*Lawrence was adamant that I not disclose the exact location of his camp.

*to go to a coffee shop and listen to the rough draft of his inter-
view. My proposal makes him very uncomfortable, because
he's afraid that there might be a woman behind the counter.
Instead we walk up to Bedford Avenue and find a laundry
mat with some tables out front.*

*Lawrence listens to his story in quiet contemplation. He
poses little issue with the content, but he is particularly insis-
tent that I change certain elements of syntax. Each time the
words "girl" and "boy" appear, he insists that I change them
to "son" and "daughter." I patiently make other changes
revolving around the word "her" and the verb to be. When we
finish reading, I ask Lawrence what he has in his plastic bags.*

There's no supermarket in Bedford, so I shop at
Key Food on Avenue D. I still get SSI and food stamps
delivered general delivery. One time I got a letter saying that I was no longer eligible because I was no
longer a member of Rockland Psychiatric Center, but
they still haven't cut off my check. I'm constantly wondering when I'm going to receive some negative letter
because I don't take my pills. They know that, because
I'm not spending my Medicaid money. If they see you
haven't seen a psychiatrist, they think that they have a
right to harass you.

The last time I talked to a psychiatrist he told me
that all my problems were sexual. That's because they
see everything on a sexual platform. They don't look
at things on a spiritual level. They have no soul at all.
They define sanity according to the Hebrew system,
but I are on the level of the ancients.

*I bump into Lawrence more frequently during spring of
2002. Gradually, he becomes more open in describing the
details of his personal life, and in June he explains to me with
great distress that the Sanitation Department bulldozed his*

shack underneath the Williamsburg Bridge. Two weeks later he tells me that social services cut off his check, because he hadn't filled the prescriptions for his psychiatric medications.

One night in early July I arrive at Tompkins Square to find MTV filming a commercial on the corner of 7th Street and Avenue A. Lawrence approaches shouting, YOU'RE RAPING THE CHILDREN!!! YOU'RE RAPING THE CHILDREN!!!! The film team is forced to turn off their cameras. Shortly after, officers emerge from a van and Lawrence withdraws to the park. When the director complains about the sexual inappropriateness of Lawrence's behavior, I proceed to call the man a hypocrite. Lawrence smiles in the distance.

The next day Lawrence finally consents to having his photo taken. As I put my camera back into my bag, I tear out his section from my manuscript and hand it to him. After glancing over it, he urgently pleads for another interview. We arrange to meet the next day, but the regulars tell me that I had missed him by minutes.

A week before my deadline I bump into Lawrence again. I'm freezing in the bitter October rain, but he refuses to enter a coffee shop. Together we sit at the chess tables as we labor over the manuscript. I had previously squeezed out the piece-meal tidbit that Lawrence had been in Butte, Montana before arriving in New York. When I question him further about his arrival, his face glows with a torrent of emotion and tears begin to flow.

I just got evicted from my Federal Housing Project in Montana. I had a friend who was from the Bronx, and we put together a puzzle of New York City. I just decided I wanted to be here. I had a 1969 Chevy Van, and we left with thirty-five dollars in our pockets and I had my two sons. No, not sons, two of my four offspring with me. I was still a born again

Christian at the time, and we stopped at churches and kitchens to get gas. I was in Newark six days later. When I drove through the Holland Tunnel the first time, I knew I never wanted to leave this place.

We drove around the city lost for about eight hours, and then we ended up at the EAU *(Emergency Assistance Unit)* on Catherine Street. Good thing it was there, because we got to sleep inside, but it was also a bad thing, because my two offspring had to go to school at IS 31 in Chinatown. They didn't like it, because they spoke Chinese in the classes. They wanted to go home, so I drove them back to Montana, then I turned around and went back to New York.

I parked my van on 8th Street. Pretty soon I started fighting my first battle. I was still under the influence of the clergy, so I spent my days scrubbing off the pentagrams that these kids drew on the buildings. Then my van ended up getting towed, and I ended up having to stay in a shelter.

I was scrutinized by social workers, and I didn't like that. One day there was this art instructor who wanted me to watch a movie about mythology. I told him that to teach myth as real is wrong, and I got angry. Four cops came in and took me to Bellevue. They wouldn't let me go.

I knew that I would never get out, because I had no next of kin. I wouldn't give them my mom's phone number, because I knew that they would call, and I didn't want my mom to go through that. So, I knew that I'd never get out.

And so I vegetated in Bellevue for I don't know how long. My conception of time came from the ice on the East River. LET ME OUT!!! LET ME OUT!!! That's all I knew. I knew that they wouldn't understand me, and, and, and I was gonna be there forever. Heh heh, I wasn't gonna get out!

When they sent me to Rockland Psychiatric Center, this social worker was trying to get me out of there. She got a hold of my lawyer in Montana, and they put me on a plane to Butte. And, and, *(sobs)* it takes so long for your brain to get off of them drugs.

When I got off the their drugs, I took a bus back to Manhattan. There was this guy in the candy store who was using all of his power on this daughter who was working in there, and I couldn't stand it. I stuck my hand in front of his eyes, and coffee went flying. He went running outside and the THE MOVIE COP, THE MOVIE COP CAME AND ARRESTED ME, AND I WENT BACK TO BELLEVUE!!!

They shot me full of drugs again, and then they sent me back to Rockland, and back to Butte, Montana on Valentines Day. Three days later, I bought a bus ticket back to New York and sat in this park for six months, and I was worthless, because I HAD ALL THOSE DRUGS IN MY BRAIN!!!

In '97 and '98 I was fine, but in '99 I got arrested on 1st Avenue, and they sent me to Riker's Island. They made me talk to a psychiatrist, and he wasn't listening at all. They took me to Elmhurst Hospital, and then to Creedmore Psychiatric Center. THEY TOOK MY 1999. THEY TOOK MY 2000 AWAY FROM ME!!! Then my son got me back to Butte Montana again.

I got on another bus and came back here January 2nd, 2001. Since then I've been in Bellevue twice. One time they kept me for seven days.

When I first started talking to you, I thought that you were trying to take me back to Bellevue. It scares me. It scares me that they can do that to another human being. But I've never told anybody this, and it feels good. I need to do this. I need to relax. I can't think of a way to say thank you. Thank you so much. What is your name?

I speak with Lawrence two more times during the final week before my deadline. The absence of my tape recorder further opens up the exchanges. Last Wednesday, I learned that Lawrence arrived in Lon Bin, Vietnam on July 19th, 1970 with the 794th Maintenance Company, US Army. He was stationed at Fire Base Buffalo shortly after the 173rd Airborne left. Lawrence was open in discussing his experiences as a mechanic, but his face grimaced when I asked him what happened when he returned to the States.

Cheneke

Mexico City, Mexico

Cheneke is not a regular at Tompkins Square. I bump into him in early July while he is playing his wooden flute with Gray Wolf on the eastern edge of the park, a central gathering point for many Hispanic regulars. Cheneke's English is crisp with a slight accent. He responds to my questions with welcoming focus.

I was born in Mexico City. That's much different than the cities on the border like Chihuahua or Tijuana. In other parts of Mexico they don't like the people from Mexico City. They call us chilangos. My family was poor. They don't believe in middle class in Mexico. If you're rich, you're rich. If you're poor, you're poor. During the harvest season we would go work in the fields, other times we made our money by selling jewelry for the tourists. My grandparents taught me how to make metal jewelry. They used to tell me stories about Pacha Mamma Hanna Pacha, the Great Spirit.

I finished high school when I was eighteen, and I went to Tijuana. I just brought the clothes on my back and my tools. I sold my jewelry to the American tourists, and I made more money than I ever made in Mexico City. That's when I started dreaming about someday selling my jewelry on the streets of New York.

It was very hard to cross the border. Immigration caught me ten times. They call me wetback, palda mojada. Each time they would send me back. The next day, I would try again. On the tenth time, I jumped on the outside of a train and rode to Los

Angeles. There were two hundred people holding on to that train. Now it is harder. A lot of people pay one thousand dollars to a "coyote" to bring them across the border. Many people die, because people will kill you for your money.

I only stayed in downtown LA for one month. I sold some jewelry, but it was very dangerous sleeping on the streets at night. There were a lot of gangas and cholos. Too much heroin and crack—mucho violencia. You had to be careful about the color of your clothes.

I met some friends from Guatemala, and we jumped on the train again and rode up to Fresno. They knew some people who got us jobs in the fields cutting apples, peaches, and plums. We would work fifteen hours a day and make two hundred and twenty-five dollars every week, but after they charge you for your rides to the field and rent, you would have one hundred and fifty dollars a week. But I was still young, and I drank some. That cost some money, but I still managed to send money back to my family. It was hard, but it was a beautiful time. I'm a good worker. I love to work.

One night I heard some of the workers say that there was better money in Georgia. I got together with my friends from Guatemala, and we bought tickets on a Greyhound all the way across the country. What they had said about Georgia was right. There was no immigration, and it was easy to find work. I cut squash, eggplant, and tobacco. They paid better there, because they'd pay you by the bucket. Seventy-five cents a bucket. Some days I could get ninety buckets. One day I got a hundred and twenty buckets in 12 hours. But they still charge you thirty dollars a week for rent, and fifty dollars a week for your ride to the field. After three years in America I sent one thousand dollars back to my family in Mexico. A lot of people say that Mexicans work hard, but they only spend their money on drinking. That isn't true.

After we were done in the fields, people would talk about New York City. They said that there were lots of jobs and lots of Spanish speaking people. I knew that I wanted to go. I saved up money for an airplane ticket, because I always wanted to fly, and I used someone else's papers. I had eight hundred dollars in my pocket. At first I rented a room uptown for a while. Right now, I've found a lot of friends downtown so I sleep out on the streets. I feel safe here, and I save money.

Sometimes there is good money selling jewelry and flutes. I have my prices. I can only go behind two or three dollars. My stuff is only the highest quality. Sometimes I can make a hundred dollars in three or four hours. Other times it's only twenty dollars. I love to see tourists.

I used to write lots of letters home to my family, but now I use email. They have a computer. Right now I'm sending my family money to buy me some land in Mexico, so that I can build a house when I go back. My family misses me, and they want me to come back. But I have family here too. I met a good girlfriend from Italia. She has two beautiful babies, two years old and four years old. Sometimes I sleep at her house. She pays me to watch her kids. She's wonderful. We've been together for seven months.

My journey hasn't just been a journey over land. It is also a journey of the spirit. I used to go to the interfaith church in the East Village. Jesus was a good Messiah, but the people don't want to listen to anything different. The Bible is good, but you have to make your own decisions. For a while I was Hare

Krishna, but what they do is only for show. They just want all of your money. But the Krishnas still respect me, because they know I am on the right path.

Lately I've been reading a lot of Krishnamurti. Some guy just handed me a book one day, and it opened my brain like a flower. It inspires me to feel real freedom in myself. He talks about opening your eyes and listening to everything. All that you have is yourself. You can't be dependent on a religion or a philosophy to tell you what to do. When people become part of a religion, they're searching for an identity. But to me, that isn't real love. Religion creates too many boundaries that isolate you from other people. That's why they are always fighting. You have to find your own path.

Everything that you do has to be done with a strong heart. That's real love. You can't be afraid in your heart. If you're afraid you can never be at peace.

I've been in New York for two years. There are some people who don't like me because of my long hair and I'm Indian, but you meet some stupid people everywhere. I've also met a lot of good people. Life is always interesting when you live day by day. I'm going to spend one more year in New York, and then I'm going back to Mexico.

They call it the American Dream. But it is not a dream, it is real. Everything is possible if you open your brain and your heart.

I speak to Cheneke again in April as he is selling his wares in front of the Astor Place Subway Station. He tells me that he has completely moved in with his girlfriend and is no longer sleeping on the street. He now has his own phone number and is doing very well.

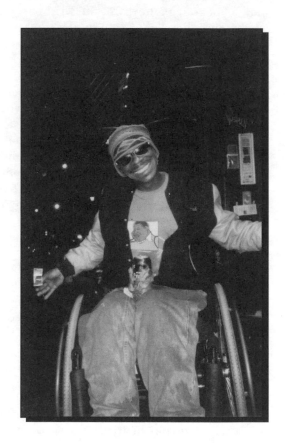

Frank

Frank casually approaches as I'm conducting another interview on Avenue C. My friend Amos takes out a guitar and begins playing softly in the background. Frank joins in with a high falsetto aimed at a parading throng of females:

I WANT YOU TO LOVE ME!!!

I WANT YOU TO LOVE ME!!!

My subject is flustered by his spontaneous harmonies. "Hey papi, we don't want you singing!"

FUCK YOU!!!

"You better watch out papi. I been a boxer four years in Dominican Republic."

You think because I'm in a wheelchair, you can whoop my ass. That's bullshit. If I get a hold of you, you're gone. I'm a strong son of a bitch. You better move quick, cause if I go over there, I'm gonna strangle you.

"Fuck you too man. Go take a walk."

I can't walk. I ain't paying you no attention, because you can walk. I been in this shit eighteen years. You lucky and you know it. Every time you see me you thank God that it's not you in this bitch. You don't know how it feels to sit in this thing . You gotta pee through a catheter. You gotta wear pampers. You get bed sores. You didn't go through that crap, so you can kiss my ass. *The first subject storms off, and Frank assumes a calmer posture.*

This wheelchair cost me five grand. She can fly like a bird. I take good care of it. I oil my axles. In Brooklyn they call me Speedy Gonzales. I'm the best. When these motherfuckers need somebody to make a store run, they send my ass.

I been out on the street for eight days. It's getting to the point where I hope the judge locks me up, because I can't live out here. My aunt let me crash for a few days, but I can't stay with her, because she lives on the fourth floor. She been crying her ass off. I'm thinking about killing myself.

I speak with Frank a few days later, and he tells me that he wants to write a book called Life on Wheels. *Frank, if you're serious, Curbside Press will help you publish it.*

Vince the Prince Hunter

Vince is involved with the Bowery Residence Committee.

If they would leave the cultural aspects of this city alone, New York would get back to being New York. I think it's good that they're cleaning up the city, but they need to find a way to do it without destroying the culture. They need more than just new construction. Maybe if the politicians would shell out some money for programs to expand on the artistic culture that's already here, the spirit of this neighborhood won't die.

Timbalero

I started playing timbales in my mother's apartment in Jacob Riis *(housing project on Avenue D)* in 1964 when I was fifteen years old. She still lives there. I'll invite you for dinner there tomorrow if you want. When I was eighteen I started playing with Hector La Valle. I played with a lot of bands.

I ain't playing no more, because my wife died. I met her dancing on Broadway and 96th Street. We went to Puerto Rico together and got married, then we moved back to New York and lived with my mother. She and my daughter got killed ten years ago. They were coming down the stairwell, and some guy put a knife into them. I always told my wife not to go out at night. She shouldn't a gone out.

I didn't want to live, and I thought about killing myself. That's how I fell into this homeless thing. I go to see my mother everyday and take showers. I get something to eat, I watch some TV, and I change my clothes. My mother is a santero, she believes in saints. Her apartment is full of them. The saints help me, but I don't want to stay there, because it makes me think of my wife.

Chris Gamble, Prince of Bums

Chris is a book vendor on Avenue A. He is also one of the best chess players in the park.

I came here in 1959 from Illinois. The neighborhood's changed three times. It changed with the hippies. Then it changed after the riots. It changed again when Giuliani came in. This time I think it's here to stay.

Back in the day, this place was a hellhole. That yellow line that runs down the middle of Avenue A was the dividing line between sanity and insanity. Over here you had drugs and shootings on the other side, you had people who went to work everyday.

Justin

Justin came to New York on a football scholarship to CW Post in '88.

Never judge people by the way they look. Somebody could look good, have the good job and apartment, and they could be the cheapest scumbag you'd ever meet. It's the guy out on the street that shares his nothing with you that has true integrity.

If they've got a hotdog, you've got a bite of hotdog.

Avery

I used to live in the park in the early nineties. I was young, and I didn't take life seriously I guess. I had just come back from upstate, and I couldn't get back into the swing of things. After a while I got tired, and about ten years ago, I decided to let go of my pride and go into a program.

It took years, but I finally got myself a place in Brooklyn. There's a lot of drugs down there, and that makes me uncomfortable. I know I can't be around that, so every once in a while I come back to Tompkins and sit down by myself and meditate. It kind of brings me back to my roots and lets me think about how my life has changed. It gives me the focus to keep struggling, because its hard to find good work right now.

Vic

I first meet Vic as he is pushing himself over the pedestrian bridge to East River Park. I offer to help him, but he insists on earning his own passage.

I grew up here on 6th Street. My father was a sergeant with Patton. He was the only Puerto Rican in the platoon. When the war was finished they came here. A few years ago I fell out of a second story window and shattered the bones in my legs. I'm in nasty pain. There was only so much the doctors could do.

I been down here a couple months. I lost my apartment. They said that the only places they got is for somebody with AIDS, but for somebody who's disabled they don't got no place. Now they want fourteen hundred dollars for an apartment here. I could go somewhere else, but I don't want to.

Lobo

Lobo is a good friend of Cheneke's.

My family was very poor. I didn't have a father, so my mother had to work. Coming here was such an opportunity. If you work here for a year even at minimum wage, you can still save up money. Then you can go back to Mexico City and start your own business, and you don't have to work for nobody else no more. I still have the dream of doing that, but I've gotten caught up with things that I know aren't good for me. I'm trying to make the right decisions.

Leroy

Leroy was evicted from a housing project in Canarsie, Brooklyn in September of 2002. He speaks in the soft subtle tones of an English scholar. Late one evening I approach him on Avenue A and ask, "How are you?"

The question isn't so much how I am. The real question is if I am, and yes, I am, so I guess I can't be that bad.

After we chat for a few minutes I ask him where's he's from.

I'm from Manhattan actually. But I've met so many people from all over the world, that I've always considered myself sort of an international person. I don't have to go abroad, because abroad comes to New York. That's also a pun, but it's true.

Leroy speaks to me for an hour about James Joyce. He is amazingly articulate, and I regret that I don't have time to conduct a more extensive interview.

Helping Hands

Very few service organizations appear to be directly involved with the people I interviewed. Most interactions that I witness revolve around securing the tangible commodities of food, clothing, clean needles, or emergency medical care. Those subjects who do seek out the human resources of social workers, counselors and therapists prefer not to talk about the experience. When I begin to meet some of these professionals, I realize that some organizations are playing a greater role than what is evident in my interviews.

Unfortunately, funding limitations have prevented me from printing the full length interviews. You can find them posted on the web at

www.curbsidepress.com

Street Life Ministries

www.streetlife.org

Reverend David Van Fleet

Street Life Ministries after operates a van that provides free lunches for people around the park.

Our basic function is to provide food, clothing, and personal care items for people who have no other means of obtaining them. A lot of people just want to come and eat. That's fine, but for those that really want to get their life back together, we're there to refer them on the spot for that type of help. Proper information and is the key for these people to utilize the available resources.

Lower East Side Harm Reduction Center/Needle Exchange

www.leshrc.org

Raquel Algarin

The LESHRC operates an outreach center at 25 Allen Street. In addition to exchanging needles, they provide counseling, holistic healing and a wide variety of other services.

Forty percent of the people who contracted AIDS last year were either infected through a shared syringe or sexual contact with someone who had shared a syringe. It would be nice if we could flip a switch and keep everyone from using drugs, but that's not reality. The philosophy of Harm Reduction is to minimize the damage that these people are exposed to. It hasn't been the most popular philosophy, but it works. Over the past twelve years we've provided services to keep thousands of people from being infected.

photo Clayton Patterson

Picture the Homeless

www.picturethehomeless.org

Anthony Williams

Anthony Williams and Lewis Haggins formed Picture the Homeless while living in Bellevue Men's Shelter in winter of 2000. The organization is made up entirely of people who are or have been homeless. This spring PTH won a lawsuit against the NYPD for specifically targeting homeless people for arrest.

Our organization is about getting actual homeless people involved in public policy. All through the city you've got people talking about the "homeless problem," but the perspective of the person on the street gets lost. See, the politicians want to portray us in a negative light to allow them to perpetuate human rights violations. They think that if they make our day to day life a living hell we'll pack up and leave. Picture the Homeless isn't going to let that happen.

Gene Rice and Warren Prince

Prince and Gene were homeless and addicted to crack for 12 years. In 1999 they overcame their addiction and are now part of the Picture the Homeless steering committee. They speak at events throughout the country. Their story (www.curbsidepress.com) is a wellspring of positivity and inspiration.

Gene: Two weeks ago we were privileged to represent Picture the Homeless at a national forum in Washington. We were some of the only people there who had actually been homeless, so hundreds of people came and listened to what we had to say. It was so crowded that people were sitting in the aisles.

Prince: My cousin and I shatter the stereotype. We're like shock troops. We got so much to tell that you'd never be able to get it all down. And not only us, but you've got thousands of other people in this city. If you really want to know what's going on out here, you've got to stop talking about us, and start talking to us.

Grand Central Neighborhood
BIGnews Street Newspaper
www.mainchance.org
Ron Grunberg

Grand Central Neighborhood operates a full service drop in center in the basement of St. Agnes Church at 147 E 43rd Street. In April of 2000 they began publishing BIGnews *and are now distributing 25,000 copies per month. Homeless and low income vendors buy copies for twenty cents and sell them on the street for a dollar.*

Lack of living wage jobs is probably the biggest cause of homelessness. *BIGnews* gives people who have trouble finding regular employment a chance to be their own boss. In the past three years we've registered over 2,000 vendors. Some have been able to use that money to get back indoors.

BIGnews also provides a unique literary outlet. Every week we run a homeless writers group, and I'm amazed by the creativity and vision of these people. *BIGnews* lets their voices be heard.

Epilogues

In spring of 2003, two years after I took my first interview, I decided that it was finally time to take this book to press. With great difficulty, I weaned myself from carrying a tape recorder. My talks with the people in the park are shorter now. I don't hand out money anymore. Nobody complains.

Nancy

Nancy still jokes around with the guys in the Living Room. She continues to be a regular at Bellevue. This summer they had to revive her from cardiac arrest with a defribulator. "Why don't they just let me lie in peace?" she says. After a few beers she likes to dance to the music that flows out of the cars on Avenue A.

Vinny

Vinny still stands like a statue by Seventh Street, looking like he's never cried in sixty-three years. In July someone stabbed him in the chest with a wooden pencil. He just stood on the corner for a few hours until Radio Rob convinced him to go to the emergency room. Vinny returned to the park in November and is roughing out the winter underground in Second Avenue subway station.

Gray Wolf

   20 months after I last spoke to Gray Wolf, he returned to the park for a weekend visit. He had successfully completed a rehabilitation program and was now reunited with his wife and daughter. He is currently putting a down payment on a house upstate.

Gray Wolf March 2003   photo: Bob Arahood

John Connors

I put off calling John's sister for a whole month after leaving him at Port Authority. Handing John that ticket had been the high point of the entire project. If he didn't get on that bus, I didn't want to know about it. But what if he did make it? I imagined listening to him crack a few jokes and maybe pass the phone around to his family. Finally, I dialed the number and awkwardly introduced myself to the woman on the other end. It was John's sister. John gave me the right number, but he didn't get on the bus.

I saw John a few days later on Ninth Avenue. At first he told me that he had a heart attack right after I left midtown, but the more we talked, the closer we came to the truth. I don't bother with a tape recorder anymore, so I can't tell you exactly what he said, but it was something about freedom and making your own choices. I understand.

Rino

Nobody knew what happened to Rino after he was taken away. I called all three hospitals in the area posing as his nephew and was unable to even find out if he had been admitted. By autumn rumors began to spread that he had passed on. I called a social worker who had been working with Rino and still couldn't get any information. A few nights later Nancy frantically approached me on the avenue and told me that Uncle Rino was no longer with us. I tried to ask her how she knew, but she was sobbing so wildly that all I could do was hold her. After what seemed like hours, I reached into my bag and pulled out Rino's photo and gave it to Nancy. She hugged me one more time, and in my heart I knew that Rino was gone.

Two months later Uncle Rino emerged from Cabrini with a cane. "They love it when I don't die." he says. I last saw him sitting on the corner of St. Marks in the middle of February. The temperature was well below zero, so I stopped a police officer on Avenue A. Rino protested at first, but after another half hour in the biting wind he agreed to let the BRC homeless outreach van take him to the shelter.

As of April I have word that Rino is living indoors with a friend in the neighborhood.

Sweet Leif

Sweet Leif has been back in the park with the same story. I waited until now to tell you that, because the other ending seemed so perfect. It's nice to think of 9/11 as a positive turning point for humanity, no matter how temporary. I haven't seen Sweet Leif lately, and I hope that her absence is of her own volition.

Skunk

Skunk has sent me a few emails. One told me about a new tattoo on her forehead. Another said that she was with child. She's now living indoors with the father and doing fine. If you want to know more, you can ask her yourself at pooppunk@yahoo.com.

Stephanie

A month after our last interview Stephanie sent me this email:

yeah were in New orleans me and bolt split up he hit me at the squat and hurt me pretty bad an d i had to go to the hospital and get 14 stitches in my lip he busted it open pretty bad and stole all my gear and and took anubis i tryed to buy him and he wouldnt let me have him and he ended up sellling him for 150 dollars fuck that ass hole

After Stephanie split with Bolt, she went back to San Francisco and got picked up for parole violation. She has since finished her sentence and is taking art classes at a community college. She no longer shoots heroin. Drop her a line at twatrot666@hotmail.com.

Bolt

Bolt returned to East River Park with another girl in summer of 2002. They got married this spring while tree sitting in Oregon. She's nineteen.

Bolt has since kicked heroin and now nurses his addictions through copious consumption of malt liquor. At first I was skeptical, but then he showed me his bulging belly to prove it. Bolt admits to having adjustment issues, but the switch has certainly made him more energetic. That morning, the sun rose over the East River to find Bolt dangling by one hand over the guardrail. I have word that he left the city two days later and is now wintering somewhere on the West Coast.

Radio Rob

During fall of 2002 Rob began to develop respiratory problems. When I last saw him at Second Avenue station in February of 2003, his hearty laugh had withered to wheezing trickle. A week later Nancy convinced him to check into the hospital. In early March Rob passed away of a collapsed lung at his parents' house in Brooklyn. Nancy attended the funeral.

Later that day, as she cried on the bench, Vinny put his arm around her and pointed at a star glimmering through the downtown haze. "There he is Nancy, he's up there now. He's saying he loves you."

Nelson Hall

Nelson resurfaced a few days after being taken away in the ambulance. He didn't remember anything about the night that he slammed his face into the pavement. As weeks passed, his attitude became increasingly negative, and his usually comic array of panhandling jingles were forsaken for satirical ploys of self-deprecation:

"WE'RE TRYING TO GET SOME MONEY TO SEND ALL THE LITTLE COLORED KIDS BACK TO AFRICA!!!"

"WE'RE COLLECTIN' MONEY TO GIVE THE PROJECTS BACK TO THE WHITE PEOPLE!!!"

"I KNOW YOU WANNA GIVE A NIGGER SOME MONEY!!!"

Other panhandlers were angry with Nelson for "blowing up their spot." Complaints about the Reverend Doctor seemed to be the main topic of conversation at the Living Room. I didn't see any physical altercations, but Nelson seemed to have a fresh cut on his face each time I saw him. I didn't even bother asking him about my laptop, because I knew that I would be writing my own epilogue.

As time wore on Nelson's constant requests for money began to put a strain on our relationship. One night in March I walked away from him to a storm of curses. The next day he didn't even remember. In my mind, I had all but given up on Nelson. Only a year ago I was fascinated by this man's perspective, but now I was taking two avenue block detours to avoid passing him on the street. It seemed that if there was anything Nelson had to teach me, I had already learned it and there was no need to be sucked into his pathetic, wallowing misery. I barely spoke with him until one night in early July.

My evening began with a visit to a charity art auction in Soho. Eager to shmooze, I decided to bring a copy of my manuscript and see if I could find any artists who wanted to contribute drawings. To make a long story short, the art was horrible and nobody would even talk to me. I trudged back toward the park spewing muffled utterances of disdain for trust fund bohemians.

The next thing I knew, I was sitting in the Living Room with the Reverend Doctor. He was sober for the moment, but a brown paper bag in his hand fore-shadowed the demise of his conversational capacity. The talk turned to art, and Nelson was Picassoing and DuChamping away. Soon he was telling me about portraits:

"You've got to draw from the inside out. There's aesthetic technique and that's important, but that's not what gives you the true essence of a person. See, a portrait isn't like a snapshot. It's a depiction of a person over a period of time. It's not just about showing one moment, it's about showing all the things that make that person who they are. It's like magic."

Eager to put Nelson to the test, I handed him a pen. The artist smiled mischievously as he made a jit-tering swipe at the cover of my manuscript, laughing at the random scribble with aloof gratification, almost as if he was challenging me to doubt the ensuing metamorphous. Slowly, my face emerged from the tangled lines. In less than five minutes, and without glasses, Nelson finished my portrait. It was the first time he had drawn anything in three years.

I returned to the park two days later armed with a sketchbook and several different pens. I was surprised that Nelson still had them in his possession at the end of the week. As days passed, word of Nelson's artistic aspirations spread through the park, and many of the regulars were eager to pose.* Nelson chattered freely with his subjects, and not once did I hear him ask them to sit still. He had given me twelve portraits by the time I left the city for a week vacation in late July.

The Antiriot of August 2002

I didn't see Nelson the first night that I returned to the park. In fact none of the people I interviewed could be found anywhere. I did find a van with a movie projector on top shining a gigantic Nike commercial on the brick walls of the Con Edison station. Maybe Bloomberg finally did clear the place out. As I headed home, I let myself hope that Nelson had checked into a detox and not yet contacted me.

When I returned the following evening, St. Marks Place was lined by large trucks filled with electrical equipment. A table dotted with paper plates stood at the entrance to the park, but in place of the usual silent line of hungry face stood a chattering crowd of clean pressed khaki. As I turned the corner, I saw a monstrous machine dangling a spotlight above the sidewalk. At the other end of the block a man was spraying the pavement with a hose connected to a

*Not all of Nelson's subjects were homeless.

tanker truck. Orange traffic cones sealed off all traffic.

"It's the new Brittany Murphy flick. You know, she was in that movie *Clueless*?" I heard a southbound gay couple explain to a passerby.

As I crossed 7th Street, a team of bright-eyed youngsters with headphones were busy trying to route pedestrians away from the sidewalk, thanking them in advance with the firm resolve of air traffic controllers. Their requests were adequate to prevent people from crossing in front of the cones, but not stern enough to thwart a crowd of curious onlookers. Being that it was after midnight, most were on their way home from local watering holes with inhibitions diminished in parallel proportion to their wallets. Loud cries projected from a crowd smelling of cologne and glowing with testosterone. A Nets jersey led me to believe that their evening began somewhere across the Hudson.

The director turned and faced the crowd, "Guys, we're going to be rolling in a second, and I'd appreciate if you could just keep quiet for one minute. Thank you, we're trying to get this done as quickly as possible so we can go home." A headphoned brunette gently slid into position and began nursing the Jersey boys into submission. Suddenly, she pleaded with the group for silence. They complied.

"Rolling!"

With the unblemished brilliance of a grapefruit smothered in DDT Miss Murphy emerged from behind a lighted screen and strode daintily across the pseudo rain drenched stretch of Avenue A. Off in the distance I heard a voice cry out through the frozen tension:

"DEEP DOWN IN THE BOTTOM OF YOUR HOL-
LYWOOD, BLACK EVIL HEART, YOU KNOW
YOU MOVIESTARS WANNA GIVE ME SOME
MONEY!!!"

Immediately, the headset coalition tuned into their
earpieces and began to re-situate their line of defense.
I took advantage of the momentary shift and slipped
through the restricted line of lights and cameras.
Nelson was firmly planted in front of the bodega
brandishing his coffee cup like a saber. He was clearly intoxicated.

"Now you all don't have to bum rush me. Just line
up alphabetically and GIVE ME SOME MONEY!!!"

Two police officers on the corner watched with
detached amusement. It was clear that the Ninth
Precinct intended to sit this one out. When the chief
of air traffic control personally approached, Nelson let
his voice drop to the pondering intellectual tone he
uses when sober. "Oh you guys were rolling? I'll be
quiet. I respect your art. I'm not stupid."

At first Nelson cooperated, but then some of his
friends began to noisily gather about the spectacle.
John Connors destroyed the next take with a shrill cat
call. Not wanting to miss out on the fun, Nelson
returned to the sidewalk and shot off his jingles with
renewed intensity. Several of the regulars from Crusty
Lane were waiting in the wings shouting proclama-
tions of encouragement.

"These are your fuckin streets!" I imagined the
word RIOT in tomorrow's headlines.

"THAT'S RIGHT. I RUN THIS SHIT AND YOU'RE NOT GOING TO TELL ME WHAT THE FUCK TO DO WITH IT!!!"

The two police officers laughed with empathy as the director coolly masked his frustration. With cunning deception, he told Nelson that if he waited by Seventh Street, they would use him as an extra in the next shot. The ploy lasted about five minutes. Nelson soon gave way to streams of encouragement from the crowd and strode back into the spotlight with indomitable resolve:

"ALL YOU MOTHAFUCKAS THINK YOU MAKING ART!!! YOU GOT ALL THIS DAMN MONEY!!! YOU GOT ALL THESE FINE BITCHES!!! BUT YOU'RE NOT TELLING ANY REAL STORIES!!! YOU'RE NOT DOING ANYTHING THAT'S GONNA MAKE PEOPLE CHANGE — YOU GOT YOUR CAMERAS TURNED THE WRONG WAY!!!"

A moment of silence followed Nelson's blazing salvo. Slowly, he turned his eyes to the people on the sidewalk and scanned the line of faces.

Somewhere inside of me I wanted to step out from the crowd and stand with Nelson on the street. If I did, I knew that others would follow.

Surely this would be a statement. But what would we be saying? That a homeless man with a paper cup has the same right to make money on a public street as a Hollywood production company? That the Lower East Side is not for sale? Or, would it just be anotherasinine stunt? Before I had a chance to collect my thoughts the director exploded at Nelson. He did not hesitate to fire back:

"I'M THE NIGGER!!! I JUST WANT TO LET YOU
KNOW THAT I AM THE N-I-G-G-E-R!!! FUCK ALL
Y'ALL MOTHAFUCKAS!!!"

Nelson stormed up the avenue past the traffic
cones. John Connors handed him a wrinkled bag, and
the Reverend Doctor proceeded to shoot holes in the
last dangling threads of his intellect with a bottle of
Colt 45.

Two hours later, when the filming was finished, a
member of the production team informed Nelson that
he was leaning against his car, Nelson silently stum-
bled off the curb and watched the tail lights melt into
the night.

He disappeared the next day.

Despite Nelson's crude demeanor, I see beauty in
the way he makes his friends laugh. Despite his artifi-
cially induced courage, I find inspiration in his intent.
Despite his despicable example, I believe that there is
knowledge in his words. Yes, the cameras are turned
the wrong way. Ultimately it's up to Nelson to free
himself from the ragged jaws of his affliction and turn
them around. If he chooses to rise to this challenge,
his battles won't be fought in front of crowds of
onlookers, but in the chasm of his own mind. If our
friend is to succeed, it will be through his own
courage.

Those of us who share his vision will have our own
victories.

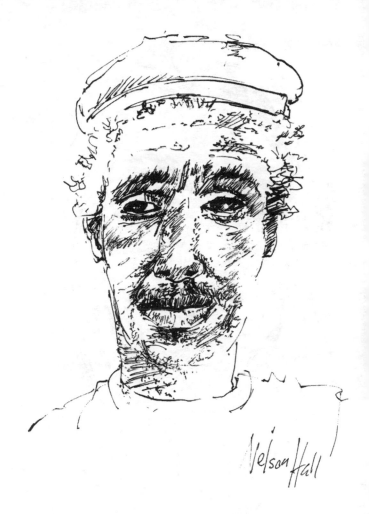

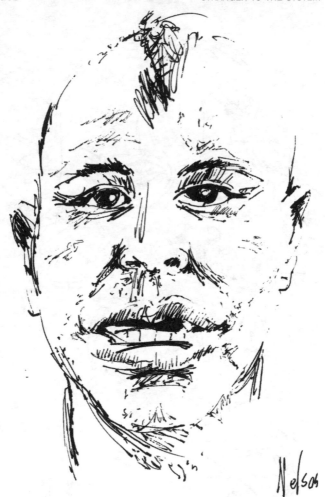

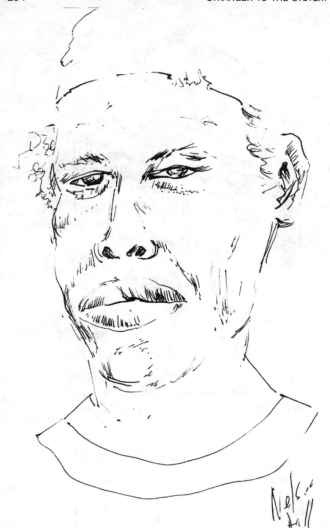

Kurt
Rest in Peace
July 2002

Resurrection

Nelson Hall

No word of Nelson was heard for three months. None of the regulars had any idea of his whereabouts, and with his absence came rumors of his demise. In early December I was overjoyed to hear a street vendor report a sighting. Apparently, Nelson had quit drinking and was living in a halfway house in Harlem. I scoured the phone book for reha-bilitation programs, but I had no luck in locating him.

Three weeks before Christmas I saw Nelson in the flesh on Avenue A entrenched in conversation with a group of reg-ulars. I immediately walked over and embraced him, but before we could speak, I had to wait for him to finish answer-ing a barrage of questions about rehab from the regulars. I listened patiently as he told them that he had spent one month in Kingsboro Detox and was now a member of Able House on Third Avenue. He hadn't so much as smoked a cigarette in ninety days. Nelson shook many hands as he spouted words of encouragement. After he had said goodbye, we stepped into a coffee house on St. Marks.

Shit. I feel like a poster boy for rehab. That's all the people out here want to talk about.

Nelson and I met the next day at the library. With a slick smile he pulled my old laptop out of a duffel bag.

Epilogue

Looking upward from the sidewalk with my cheek above the green and yellow bile that had erupted from my stomach for the sixth or seventh time that day, I could see two faces leaning down towards my anguish. As if dreaming, two strangers lifted my tired flesh into the stretcher: another body on the Bowery, vacant of vitality or hope.

"Do you have Medicaid?"

"Yes. Take me to a detox."

Take me to that detox in the sky!

Ninety days have grinded past since my last ambulance ride, my last drink, my last passage through the wilderness of self-induced amnesia. It seems easier this time, because I've truly hit rock bottom. As I look forward, I look back, for fear I might repeat the same mistakes. Tonight, hindsight finds me gazing at the patchwork of my muddled life.

Time has slipped away like silk. It seems that I can scarcely grasp the bits of my folly and faded fragments of my functionality. I remember walking wearily down the streets of haunted memories, proclaiming nothing but the inalienable human right to be insane. I hardly knew that I was naked, 'til I felt the rain of tears, the wind that turned them into ice before the eyes of those who watched me from the comfort of cozy cafes and bustling bars. I can understand their fear, their shun, their hatred and disgust at me.

But through it all, I have been my own fiercest enemy. I had let myself become so low, so utterly entrenched in morbid fatality and funk. Yet I willingly embraced it. I'd drowned myself each day and night with calculated slow intent. What external foe would have the time, the dedicated focus, and complete malevolence towards another?

I may never know the answers to these questions. I awaken to find that I'm uncomfortable, a stranger in the cloak of my own skin. For now it's better to let these ghosts disintegrate and think about the here and now, the new foundation.

The die has not been cast, and I cannot say for certain where this path will take me. I do know that whatever is to come about will be by discipline and diligent commitment. There's no compromise, no altering what's etched into the DNA of stone cold reality, the absolute conscription of the jagged bottom line of the parks, the subway stations, the shelters and halfway houses of our lives. It's a bitter and barbaric driven bargain, but somebody's got to pay. The stakes are high as life itself or brutal unto death. And frankly, I can't choose to lose no more.

To all the people living on the edge,
dying under blankets in the street
To all the people who can't compromise,
the people who say no.
To all the ones who thought they were
the baddest or the best,
To all the ones who knew they'd never be
the least impressed,
To all of you who thought you'd
never have to think at all,
Life ain't always fair, but fare you well.

To the rest of you
who've dared to decipher the madness,
Inscribed with true chaos to the core.
You have your key.
Go find your door.

As of April 2003 Nelson is still living at Able House. Despite recent budget cuts, he remains hopeful that he will find a program that will sponsor him to become a certified substance abuse counselor.

Nelson can be contacted at nelson@curbsidepress.com

Curbside Press
The Straight Up Word
From the Low Down Curb

When I first began recording in the park, I didn't give much thought to how I would present my finished product to the public. The long afternoons glued to a bench, scouring for mental clarity amid a raging sea of scattered thoughts gave little time to worry about the practical aspects of distribution. Reading from a scribbled manuscript and glancing up into a solitary pair of eyes was audience enough.

I look back with fond remembrance on the magical summer of 2001 when I listened to tapes on my roof until the Brooklyn dawn came slipping through my notebook. I now realize that the serene awakening of these moments were the true reward for my efforts. When I was frustrated and depressed, the ethereal comforts of this blessing never failed to bring me peace. I am forever grateful to those who have shared this gift, and it is only fair to give them something in return.

In the spring of 2002 I began to seriously investigate my options for publishing. Rather than submit myself to the whorish whims of the mainstream press, I applied for grants from a bevy of nonprofit organizations seeking funding to self-publish. In my proposal I detailed a plan that would provide jobs for the storytellers as book vendors. With high hopes I set out for the post office. Three months later, my refrigerator was plastered with rejection notices.

The people in the park eagerly await my promise of jobs. I have broken countless self-imposed deadlines, and we are all growing tired of waiting. Slowly, I have come to the realization that money talks, and the rest walks. I'm certainly not a loyal subject, but I do recognize the unavoidable fact that cash is king.

Having exhausted my last hopes for a grant, a week ago I went on line and applied for a $10,000 loan. Today I'm writing a check to cover the first print run. Anyone is welcome to become a vendor, provided that they follow certain guidelines. (See our web site for the rules of conduct.) Vendors will be expected to be courteous, but they will certainly be encouraged to speak out. They are no longer panhandlers of pity, but vendors of voice. The true story of these pages has only just begun. Thank you for giving us hope.

Cause we love it — when there's plenty of it.

Curbside Press is seeking:
- Volunteers to distribute books to vendors
- Web designers
- Other writers with socially relevant works
- Economical rooms for rent in NYC or NJ
- Tax deductible donations (channeled through our sponsor organization)

For information on how to become a vendor
or to volunteer call
212-251-1914
or visit our web site at
www.curbsidepress.com

About the Author

Jim Flynn is a relocated suburban kid born in Albany, New York 1977. He has taught in Manhattan public schools for the past four years and is currently a proud member of the special education department at High School for the Humanities. In November of 2001 a baseball bat-wielding landlord kicked him out of his room for rent in the Lower East Side, and he has since resided in Brooklyn. His first album, *I'm Not Sorry That I Didn't Get All GQ For Your Party,* will be released in summer of 2003. Listen at www.mp3.com.

Flynn's next project is a collection of the funniest stories in NYC titled *City of Laughter*. Give him a call if you've got a story that might work. He is also seeking speaking engagements and opportunities to freelance.

Oh yeah, anybody know of a good sublet in the LES?

jim@curbsidepress.com
212-251-1914

To listen to the music that inspired this book search for Lonesome Crew at www.mp3.com

Acknowledgments

Special Thanks to Liz and Nick Polizzi, Clayton Patterson, Ron Grunberg, Beverly Faison, Ma and Pa

Able House, alt.coffee, Aileen, American Indian Community House, Bob Arahood, Jared Bartels, BIGnews, Blue Devils JV Football, PJ Brendese, Brer Brian, Bowery Residence Committee, Matt Carlson, Spencer Chakedis, Lightnin Dan, Kimya Dawson, The Devines, Mara Drew, Joe Driscoll, Andre Dune, Curtis Eller, Electric Mind Control Workshop, Quankmeyer Fairgoalzlia, The Flynn Tribe, Scott Fragolla, State University of Geneseo, Adam Greene, Anders Griffen, HHS Class of 2003, Ange Hard-Howman, Laura Hoch, Johnny Holmes, The Hummels, Housing Works, Lilya Imas, Crazy Jay, Aisha Joseph, Bernard King, Jonathan Kozol, David Lachov, B. LaRoe, State Street Laura, Jeff and Jack Lewis, Matt Lindstrom, Eric Lippy, Sylvia Mann, Ish Marquez, Nolan McFadden, Tyler Miller, Rev. Frank Morales, Nuyorican Poets Cafe, The Persons, Brian Pilton, The Prockups, Ra Ra, The Rainbow Tribe, Raven Ministries, Ray's Candy Store, Grey Revell, Matt Rocker, Monica Samalot, Kathleen Sardo, See Squat, Sidewalk Cafe, Robby Slaughter, Langhorne Slim, Deb Smith, Lee Stringer, James Telfur, Studs Terkel, Tompkins Square Library, Mike Torpe, Amos Torres, Trinity Church, University of the Streets, The Village Chess Shop, Kurt Vonnegut, Washington Square Yeshiva, WBAI, Tom Xenakis, Liisa Yonker